HYDROPONICS FOR BEGINNERS

The Ultimate Guide To Start Growing Vegetables, Fruits And Herbs At Home Without Soil

Matthew Colery

Table of contents

CHAPTER ONE

The History of Hydroponics

Introduction

Hydroponics entails the technology of cultivating different crops without necessarily having to use the commonly known medium for growing plants, which is soil. With hydroponics, crops are planted in water richly supplied with plant nutrients, oxygen and other minerals necessary for their growth. This fact contradicts the misconception that plants only can grow in soil. To appreciate this technology, one needs to understand its history and origin.

The origin of hydroponics

The history of hydroponics dates far back to the 1600s, thousands of years ago though it sounds more like modern technology. The genesis of this fantastic technology stems nearly to the origin of the earth. The practice of cultivating with photosynthetic algae and bacteria photosynthetically was already in place way before terrestrial plants, which ideally would purify the surrounding environment.

As far as 500 BC, the famous hanging garden established by King Nebuchadnezzar II of Babylon was already in place. By this age, there were already seven wonders of the ancient world, including the intricate watering system that rendered support to enormous gardens. To these gardens, water rich in essential plant nutrients was supplied from a water reservoir strategically located to feed all the gardens at any one time. To ensure the healthy growth of these crops, the oxygenated water supply was consistently maintained.

In the year 1600, a Belgian scientist called Jan Van Helmond made the earliest scientific attempt to investigate plant nutrients critically essential for crop growth. He experimented to find out substances in water that could support plant life without soil. In his experiment, he used a five-pound of willow shoot, which he placed in a tube with two hundred pounds of soil. To enable accuracy of the result, he isolated the soil for five years while consistently spraying the soil with rainwater. He discovered that the willow shot gained weight by one hundred sixty pounds, whereas the weight loss of the soil was only by two ounces. The experiment led him to conclude that plants are the right plants that draw nutrients from the water, which can support their survival, though he did not consider the fact that plants need carbon dioxide and oxygen as well.

In the 17th and 18th centuries, scientific research gained traction and momentum into more discoveries as to necessary nutrient requirements that can support plant growth using the modern theory of chemistry. Scientists in this error showed the ability to agree on a unified system to investigate the vital essentials for crop survival. The conception of the new plant growth requirement dates back to this period.

Several experiments were conducted by scientists in the mid 19th century to uncover the composition of plants and their needs. In their tests, they were able to realize that soil alone is not sufficient or directly linked to plant growth except offer a firm position and keep the necessary crop minerals. The discovery revealed that soil plays the role of keeping the minerals, nutrients incorporated into it. The soil also offered space between for free circulation of oxygen crucial for crop survival.

Next on the scientist's list was the need to replace the soil, which they simply referred to as growing medium for plants. They successfully replaced soil with water solution richly supplied with all plant nutrients and minerals deemed vital for crop growth.

The Ancient Far East: Far long ago, rice and other plants in Asia were dominantly cultivated using hydroponic technology. In the beginning, there emerged trials to grow rice in soil. It was intercepted by difficulties in scaling up when there turned to be more market for rice, making it a substantial investment. The hydroponic technology gained traction after the destruction of other alternative crops by major seasonal flooding where only rice surviving in the waterlogged condition. The survival of rice in the waterlogged condition paved the way for hydroponic rice farming to gain momentum up today. After this incident, water systems were globally developed to grow rice, which led to an overall boost in rice production due to better control of pests and diseases.
It is equally imperative to note that due to the boost in rice production, there was a substantial shift from using hydroponics for rice farming only to farming other types of food. Later, fish farming was also practiced within the waters in rice paddies meant for crop farming. The Chinese even became more creative, and further transformed hydroponics from rice farming to aesthetic pleasure inform of platform floating gardens for recreational purposes.

Tiberius: Around the first century, Archaeologists had already established that the Roman Emperor Tiberius used the most sophisticated hydroponics at that time in the world successfully. The emperor cultivated cucumbers for a season using hydroponic technology before it became a standard farming method. To the Romans, it was the "clear stones" through which the plants grew and being supplied with essential plant nutrients. Though it was not established what those "clear stones" were, it could have probably been aiding plant growth in their time.

There was also a debate about the term "translucent stone" as regards to what it means. There were thoughts that it is a growing medium, an equivalent of soil. Later, though strange, the "translucent stone" was an ancient form of a greenhouse where a clear stone was used as a material. The greenhouse technology was discovered because there was a need to have enough sunlight, heat, and stored humidity to grow cucumber in its offseason.

The Aztecs: The Aztecs per harps played a significant role in the civilization of hydroponics, which cannot be ignored in understanding its history. The significance in their development of hydroponics was ignited by the fact that they were nomads and the nature of their environment characterized by swamps, marshy lands. The Aztec generally did not have suitable arable land for farming to support their population and their livestock. This necessitated them to create effective hydroponic systems to grow crops to support their survival.

Due to the swampy, marshy lands of the Aztecs, they designed the hydroponic system to float on water, which others called a floating raft farm. The floating raft was made out of reeds and rushes that had dried hard roots making then dense. In a floating manner, the barge would float with the crops within their settlement in the canal. The crops penetrated their roots past the rafts below to access water, and the plants obtained nutrients from the silt or the bottom of the channel. Such a system effectively substituted farming on land.

Chinampas was the name accorded to these rafts. It was amazing that these chinampas did not sink despite the heavyweight of the crops, including trees that were grown on it. The free capacity of the Chinampas was so strong primarily because it was carefully constructed out of stalks and strong hard roots. Loaded with sediments, the tough roots were tied together. The crops drew their nutrients from the deposits that had an abundance of organic minerals and consistent water from beneath the floating raft that enabled the plants such as vegetables, flowers to thrive.

The Aztecs could join the chinampas as long as two hundred feet to form floating islands properly constructed with waterways and drainage systems integrated with it. But most interesting was the provision of the caretaker's residence within the chinampas. The convenience of creating the gardener's home within the chinampas allowed him to only pull the chinampas to the shore of the river on market days to quickly sell his vegetable and flowers to buyers while on the raft. How interesting

At that time, the Aztecs were known to have provided great civilization to over two hundred thousand people using the chinampas. The success of the Aztecs sparked off other inventions such as the horticulture system in Central Mexico, providing a farming alternative for the city population. It was the beginning of the full spread of efficient farming without soil.

The chinampas were practiced until the 19th century. Countries such as Ecuador, Peru, Bolivia, among others, used the chinampas system of the farming way before Columbus in the new world. Such a system is still evident in Xochimilco and southwest Tlaxcala state in Mexico.

The beginning of the developments of modern hydroponics

The start of the development of modern hydroponics can be traced back to different explorers from around the world. In Spain and China, the practice of hydroponics civilization was properly documented explored were noticed by Conquistadors and Christopher Columbus, respectively.

Hydroponic technology, which seems modern, started with trials to properly comprehend the technology in scientific analytics. In the ancient age, hydroponics technology was already being practiced with success. The crucial difference between ancients and modern hydroponics is only the experimental analysis, which has made advanced hydroponics more quantifiable. The capacity and capability to modify, analyze current hydroponic systems, and more discovery of plant growth boosters was the genesis of modern hydroponics.

Early ideas that elevated hydroponics

Known to be the mastermind, Leonardo Da Vinci was faster than his time, and he foresaw the possibility of plant growth as he worked for King Francis, a French King. Leonard Da Vinci continued to pursue his agricultural studies. Consequently, he discovered that plants could not thrive and survive without absorbing certain minerals and other plant nutrients from the soil. He was able to figure out that water's presence necessitated the movement and transportation of these minerals and nutrients from the ground to plants through absorption.

Much as modern scientists upheld his discovery after a long time probably hundreds of years, and he cannot be forgotten because he laid absolute foundation and platform for what hydroponics is today. He was able to analyze and point out the full scope of substantial use of irrigation, which up to this present-day constitutes the crucial principles in the application of modern hydroponics. Among the fantastic discoveries that earned him much credit included administering minerals to plants in water solution, soilless farming, extensive benefits of irrigation, plants' ability to absorb minerals and nutrients from water solution.

Significant developments in hydroponic technology between 1600-1800

The adverse weather conditions and the need to scale up farming back in the 1600s drove people to start attempts to develop cultivation systems that were far better than the practices they had. These developments were not entirely hydroponic, though; they pulled interests in creating better methods for growing plants.

Farming in a soilless condition was published in a book written by Sir Francis Bacon. The book was known to have taken the first title about hydroponic technology. On a sad note, Sir Francis Bacon did not live up to the publicity of his book; he died in 1627 before it was published, but many of the scientific researchers benefited from his book after that.

There were no other significant discoveries that occurred after the death of Sir Francis Bacon until 1699 when Woodward experimented in a soilless environment using spearmint. The outcomes of his investigation revealed that plants grew better in impure water as opposed to growing plants in distilled water.

Again, the century that followed (1700) went on without having particular experimental trials on hydroponics technology. The experiments in this period per harps led to the invention of several greenhouses that relied on heated manure; it can be related to modern hydroponic technology that uses heat.

Until 1860, Julius Von Sachs, a university professor, discovered a standard formula that contained a blend of various plant nutrients with the ability to dissolve when subjected to a humid condition capable of supporting plant growth. He called it "Nutriculture."

In these early findings, it was revealed that average plant growth is a higher possibility, mainly when plant roots are introduced in a water solution that has a combination of salts such as Nitrogen, Potassium, Magnesium, among others. The reaction between air and water produces Hydrogen, Oxygen, and Carbon, without which plant growth is impossible, whether in water or soil. Further laboratory investigations by scientists in this error showed that in small quantities, elements such as Zinc, Copper, Boron, and Manganese are also required by the plant to survive. In total, scientists came up with a list of nine elements essential for plant growth.

However, in this period, the practicability of these discoveries did not pick interest not until 1925 after the growth of the greenhouse industry. Although the greenhouse industry applied nutriculture, it faced a massive challenge of changing the soil more often to preserve soil structure, maintain soil fertility, and reduce the chances of spreading pests and diseases. Soilless farming avoided all these challenges

Hydroponic developments in the 19th century: Scientists, after some centuries, put together various aspects of hydroponic technology in the pursuit to comprehend further. They had begun to grasp the technology better, and many of the findings were in the 1800s, which makes it safe to say that this period paved the path to hydroponic technology development. It was also within this period that a list of nine elements was developed capable of supporting plant life in the absence of soil. Much as these nine minerals were not so perfect as it should appear, it was a step closer to concluding that plants could be sustained without soil. Provided these minerals can adequately supply the crops in the right quantities at the stipulated time interval.

The nine minerals were further investigated by Jean Baptiste Boussingault, a scientist who somewhat confirmed these elements, which were identified to be of vital importance to plant survival. In 1851, Baptiste experimented with this using soil-like material in which he introduced the plants. He used materials such as black charcoal, quartz as well as the pure sand. Baptiste consequently supplied the plants with a chemical solution that contained minerals. In his experiment, he identified nitrogen as a required nutrient for plant survival. However,

Baptiste proceeded to establish the correct proportions and ratios of these required mineral solutions just enough to sustain plant life.

Per harps Baptiste's discovery in this age was the last as there were no other findings in this period as regards to hydroponic studies until 1900. The revelations in this age, however, played a significant role in establishing a firm foundation in the creation of good plant food such as fertilizer used in hydroponics in the present day.

Hydroponic developments in the 20th century:
From the 1920s to 1930s, soilless culture was already being spear by scientist Dr. Victor Tiedjens. Dr. Tiedjens realized that fertilizer farmers used to boost plant growth were in solid form and noticed that plants could only utilize the fertilizer in liquid form through absorption using their roots. He amazingly analyzed and figured out that plants could absorb whole lots of other dry materials if they were dissolved in water solution. Plants could make better use of mineral nutrients in these dry materials through absorption. This was a breakthrough in the use of liquid fertilizers.

To achieve better efficiency, Dr. Tiedjens surpassed applying fertilizers in the soil but instead started introducing liquid fertilizer straight on the plants. This laid the basis for folia nutrition. It did not gain traction until the discovery of high-grade raw materials that could alternatively be substituted with natural elements present in non-liquid fertilizers.

Dr. William F. Gericke, in 1929, turned his laboratory where he investigated nutriculture into a crop production center on a commercialized scale. He referred to his nutriculture technology as "hydroponic." Hydroponic is a Greek term that can be broken down into hydro, meaning, "water," Ponos meaning, "work." His work was a big success to the extent that newspapers published it as a revolutionary development in agriculture, showing him gathering his tomato fruit in his twenty-five-foot garden.

Unfortunately, Dr. Gericke's success and the publication of the news by the press gave rise to false market selling fake hydroponic types of equipment. The population took advantage of this development, thus diluting the market with counterfeit products, causing more harm. This slowed down the growth of hydroponic technology for years.

In 1938, two scientists Daniel Armon and Dennis Hoagland furthered experiments initially carried out by Dr. Gericke on the ideology of soilless culture. They recorded and published the results of their investigation that became the foundation of hydroponics. In their documentation, they recorded proven chemical solutions with formulas for the nutrients and minerals, which they referred to as Hoagland solution, which are still extant. Subsequently, this paved the way for the commercialization of hydroponics. It was also noted that employees of Pan-Am airline fed on vegetables planted using this soilless technology. Their publication was titled "The water culture method for growing plants without soil."

A continuous curiosity among the scientists and federal governments rejuvenated further investigation of hydroponic technology when governments started sponsoring scientific experiments in 1939 during World War II. The British Army, together with America's Army, relied on food harvested using hydroponic technology. Both governments established hydroponic farms at their military camps on which they cultivated plants enough to sustain their forces to fight in World War II. Hydroponics later after World War II remained the central food production technology employed by the troops, whereas in America, new food production using hydroponic technology expanded up to eight million pounds by 1952. High demands for fresh food influenced massive such output, Iwo Jima, Guyana, and Ascension Islands were among other military camps where hydroponic operations registered the most top success.

Before the popularity of hydroponic technology, there were set of drawbacks such as poor farming techniques, the use of inferior materials, and rudimental environment controls. The constructed iron pipelines that supplied liquid plant minerals and nutrients rusted, toxin levels increased as beds made out of concrete outlived their usefulness, thereby contaminating liquid plant minerals fed to the crops. However, in the mid 20th century, all these challenges were successfully overcome.

In the 1970s, plastics became standard, which substituted the hazardous parts of the old systems and was affordable to construct hydroponic systems. Consequently, this led to the adoption of hydroponic technology as the most viable cultivation technique. The shift to the use of plastics led to the manufacturing of water pumps, plastic plumbing types of equipment, timers, and computerized automation of growing media. At this point, people could personalize hydroponic systems and commercialize it due to the cost-effectiveness of the new system.

Contemporary Hydroponics

The basis of contemporary hydroponics can be traced far back into history, which has numerous hydroponic civilizations. Hydroponics today is more advanced with sophisticated technology opposed to simple traditional hydroponics. Although hydroponics today is a little complicated, its crucial purpose today is the same as it was in ancient times. The basic of hydroponics, which is growing plants in water instead of soil, has equally remained the same. Contemporary hydroponics involves the use of superior technology, but it all relies on water or the use of liquid mineral solutions.

More extensive studies and investigation have led to more modern hydroponics upgrades than ancient hydroponic technology. The new developments and improvements in contemporary hydroponics range from equipment upgrades such as timers, monitoring mineral levels, computations for proper tower spacing to discovering other growth mediums.

Today, the advancements in technology have multiplied efficiency in hydroponics, consequently leading to the development of new types of hydroponic systems such as aeroponics. The current technological capacity has further led to the emergence of eco-friendly greenhouse techniques referred to as plant factories. These advances have enabled the practice of hydroponics in homes for growing fruits and vegetables.

Hydroponics in the future

Hydroponics has had a series of revolutions through thousands of years up today. This revolution impacted several cultures with favorable results through history up to date.

It is essential to acknowledge the great explorations and developments in hydroponics over the past centuries. Considering massive and consistent events of hydroponics from ancient times up to date, it is expected that hydroponic technology still has a high potential for further renovations and improvements as it had been witnessed with other technologies like aerospace.

Therefore, it is possible to witness an influx of more effective and efficient methods of hydroponic. Benefits associated with hydroponics such as environmental conservation, the boost in agricultural production has raised global hopes that hydroponics is most expected to gain full momentum to replace traditional soil farming. Human curiosity has always supported and shaped innovations throughout history. Curiosity will certainly drive societies to invent better technologies that can make life easy and sustainable, thereby increasing the possibility of efficient hydroponic technology in the future.

CHAPTER TWO

What Hydroponics Does, How Hydroponics Works, Choice of plants

What does hydroponics do?

As discussed earlier at the beginning of this book in chapter one, we said hydroponics simply involves a soilless culture of cultivating various types of plants. The variety of crops grown using this technology range from vegetables, fruits to flowers, herbs, and cereals such as rice growing in ancients the Far East using water as the medium for plant growth. Hydroponic technology is known to have boosted crop production by aiding rapid plant growth. The faster plant production is mainly because of the supply of all the requirements vital for plant growth, especially plant minerals and nutrients fed through water solution directly to the plant roots allowing easy absorption.

Soil as a medium for plant growth, was investigated by scientists to only hold plants firmly in position, letting crop roots search the minerals needed for their growth. Hydroponics technology saves plants from the stress of penetrating the soil structure in search of nutrients, oxygen, and water to sustain their life. This also allows plants to utilize the extra energy for maturation instead of using it for soil penetration. This explains why plants nourish faster and yield better in a hydroponic system.

The hydroponic system is also known for space utilization, as it does not need extensive farmland to grow crops compared to the use of field farms that requires a big space for cultivation. Hydroponic farms are designed to consume little recyclable amounts of water than traditional gardens.

It is a solution well-balanced with plant minerals such as nitrogen, calcium, magnesium, sulphur, and other elements like oxygen; carbon dioxide is introduced to the plants according to that plant's requirements. Hydroponic systems call for some degree of expertise as to what and how much water and plant nutrients need to be proportionate to the crop requirements. The application of fewer plant nutrients and minerals will affect the plant's growth more so the total yield. Overuse may as well suffocate and affect their return too. Therefore, the proportionate application of these nutrients is paramount.

The hydroponic system's holistic operation is derived from the need to support the ever-surging world's population and the rapid demise of arable land due to atmospheric degradation by manufacturing industries. The hydroponic system works to offer an alternatively affordable platform for agriculture to sustain the growing population. Plants are already being cultivated on rooftops and house verandas hydroponically. Through the hydroponic system of cultivation, the prevalence of pests and diseases has been eliminated in totality. What hydroponic technology therefore does is the utilization of every little space for farming, fostering plant growth, increase plant production, offers complete control of plant growth because the system allows for the feeding of plant nutrients, minerals, oxygen, and carbon dioxide without which plant survival is impossible.

How hydroponics works

While designing hydroponic systems right from ancient times by various scientists, they considered many aspects, including the fact that plants manufacture their food by a process called photosynthesis. They further realized that this process requires sunlight, carbon dioxide, oxygen, and chlorophyll. The light acts as a source of energy or fuel for that matter, which helps to break molecules of water absorbed by roots. Hydrogen and carbon dioxide mixed will react to form carbohydrates that give plants better nourishment. When all the critical plant growth requirements are applied to the plant roots through water, plants can be better nourished within the shortest period possible.

Total control of conditions such as pH balance, temperatures, light, and efficient utilization of water and minerals explain how hydroponic technology functions. That said, hydroponic systems work under simplified basics like how much nutrients do particular plants need, what nutrients do they need to thrive and survive. It allows effective control of the environmental elements and full customization of every plant requirement to speed up growth. Modern hydroponic systems such as EBB and Flow system has a timer to control the water flow from the reservoir to the plants.

Comprehensive management of a hydroponic environment minimizes the number of risk factors. Outdoor field farming conventional in traditional cultivation exposes plants to a whole set of variables that can adversely affect plant growth and health. Variables such as wildlife, especially rodents, can eat up plants, locusts among other many pests can manifest and plunder plants on the farm, thus affecting crop yield. Soil as a medium facilitates the growth of fungus that breeds disease and spreads it to the crops. With hydroponic systems, plant growth can be forecasted and predicted as pests are controlled, the right proportion of plant nutrients are supplied to their roots, soil resistance to root penetration is eliminated, leading to the production of better-quality yields.

A brief look at the types of hydroponic system

Several different techniques of growing plants hydroponically are used depending on the individual choice of plants to cultivate. The various systems of hydroponics include.

- Nutrient Film Technique – This involves using a conveyor like a system that transports the liquid containing the nutrients by sliding beyond plant roots placed in troughs, which are plastic.
- Deep Water Culture System – Here, aerated water solution is used over which plants are suspended in net pots above the water source.
- Wick systems – this system works by a process called a capillary. A tray is rested on the water source containing dissolved plant nutrients. The wicks move from the reservoir to the tray in which the plants are grown.
- Ebb and Flow Systems – This system uses a timer that controls the pump by allowing water to flood the plant bed with minerals in the reservoir under when the timer is on, and the flow stops immediately when the timer stops.
- Drip System – Drip system lets aerated reservoir with a nutrient water solution to be pumped via inter-connected tubes to single plants. The water is dropped to plant roots to moisturize them.
- Aeroponics system – Unlike other systems, here plant roots are hanged in the air, introducing them to mist containing required nutrients.

Theoretically, any crop could grow in hydroponic technology though others would, of course, yield well just like in traditional farming. Vegetables like tomatoes, eggplants, and fruits such as strawberries are examples of plants that can grow better hydroponically.

Step by step guide to growing plants hydroponically

Identify hydroponic cultivation sites: A hydroponic system can be situated in a closed structure; a greenhouse is a typical example or a basement. Perfectly planned outdoor platforms could also work as well as balconies or verandas. The greenhouse floor must be evenly levelled to make certain plant nutrients equally distributed to all plants. If an individual chooses to cultivate in an open area, defensive barriers should be established to protect the system and plants from environmental disasters such as strong winds that can destroy the system. Water levels should also be monitored closely in an outdoor setting, as more water could be lost through evaporation. The additional lighting system must be in place if a person prefers to set his hydroponic system in-house.

Set the hydroponic system: Scientists developed numerous magnificent hydroponic systems from which a person can choose according to their needs. These systems include Nutrient Film System, Deep Water Culture System, Drip System, Aeroponic System, Wick System, Ebb, and Flow System, among others, as we shall discover in chapter four. Suppose we are using Nutrient Film System. Get about six PVC pipes (tubes), trellis and a stand, a nutrient reservoir, a water pump, lastly, a chamber with several openings. Place the water pump inside the tank containing the nutrients just right below the PVC tubes.

The water pump is placed inside the reservoir for it to push plant minerals. The tubes will lead the nutrients to individual plants through manifolds. The nutrients are supplied to the plants after pressure has built in the manifest shooting the minerals to the plants via small tubes. As the pressure pulls the nutrients to the plant roots, bubbled air is formed, providing sufficient oxygen to the plants. The water in this system is drained back to the reservoir using the tubes.

Mix plant nutrients in the water tank: After identifying which plant to grow, determine the exact plant nutrient requirements for that crop, you have identified it to grow hydroponically. Mix the nutrients proportionately to ensure faster growth and higher yield. Begin to operationalize the system firstly by turning the pump on for about thirty minutes. This allows for proper mixing of plant nutrients and minerals.

Introduce plants to the ready set up growing tubes: Planting seeds directly into the hydroponic garden is not convenient at all. But instead, use already germinated seeds or buy them in case you cannot grow the seeds into seedlings, thereby saving time. If you decide to buy the seedlings, select the healthiest of all. Clean the seedlings of soil and any other dirt or impurities on the roots that will affect the number of plant nutrients in the water solution. This can be done by fixing the roots in a cool or slightly warm water *(too cold and warm water can lead to plant shock)*. In a gently careful manner, the roots should be separated to avoid twisting and allow proper cleaning; otherwise, any soil particle that remains could block the spray tubes, interfering with sufficient nutrient supply.

After thoroughly cleaning the roots, reach the roots to the nutrient water solution by pulling them up to the bottom. To firmly hold the plants to a position, use pebbles of clay soil, which has been expanded. Make sure the stones are not burdensome; otherwise, it could destroy plant roots.

Tie or clip the plants to the wooden or metal bars (trellis): To prevent bending and falling of the plants, hold them onto the trellis by clipping or tying using a rope. Wind creeping plants gently onto the trellis from the base to the top. This ensures the upright growth of the plants by offering firm support to their week stems.

Switch on the pump in the reservoir and supervise the system every day: Depending on the location of the hydroponic farm, water levels should be monitored daily. It can be checked twice or thrice in drier and hot areas where the evaporation rate is much higher compared to areas with cold temperatures. It is paramount to schedule monitoring of pH and mineral levels to effect proper plant growth.

As we all know, in a hydroponic setting, all vital plant nutrients and minerals dissolve in a solvent and fed to the plant, including oxygen, to sustain their growth. The plants can become malnourished should the nutrient levels drop below the desired amount. Therefore, monitoring the nutrient and water level in the reservoir is very critical.

Monitor crop growth and watch out for pests and diseases: Because plants have all the necessary nutrients and water, their rate of growth is faster. With such a rapid growth rate, plants will cover the trellis within weeks. Close monitoring and supervision of the plants can prevent overcrowding and suffocation.

Keenly pay attention to the symptoms of pests and diseases. Pests could have eaten leaves with holes. Spot out unhealthy crops and uproot them away. Like a contagious disease, plant disease can spread from one plant to another, thereby infecting the rest of the plants due to nearness. Hydroponically grown crops do not need to penetrate the soil as nutrients are already fed directly to the roots. The energy they would have used to penetrate soil is reserved for their growth and fight diseases. Much as hydroponics limits plant exposure to pests and diseases, they still have to be supervised closely because, at any one point, they can be prone to pests and diseases.

Why hydroponics?

Implementing a hydroponic system to some extend requires specialty compared to traditional gardening, which people have survived on for several thousands of years. Yet hydroponics has continued to gain traction. It is noted that many people around the world are changing to using hydroponics as a method of cultivation because of the benefits it has over traditional gardening method.

First and foremost, traditional farming cannot be practiced in a desert-like area of the world, such as the Kalahari Desert in southern Africa, arid regions of Israel. These areas survive on the locally produced food produced hydroponically. Equally, hydroponics is practicable in overpopulated places, typically cities and town where there is limited land for agricultural activities and even the available land are expensive to acquire. Areas like Russia, Alaska, among others that receive little or no sunlight, leaves people with no choice except practicing hydroponic farming as temperature and light can be regulated.

Traditional farming involves clearing land through deforestation, which causes desertification and the loss of animal and plant habitat. That said it is inevitable to use hydroponic technology because of the positive environmental impacts such as water conservation and the reduction of various emissions in the atmosphere. The faster growth of hydroponic plants has increased food production, which in turn has lowered food prices and improved access to food. This means harvest time has also been shortened

Despite all the significant benefits of hydroponics, it has not become as popular as it should have because of some disadvantages it has. This will be discussed in the later chapters.

Choice of plants for hydroponics

Various plants thrive differently in each hydroponic system. The following aspects can help you to correctly choice the type of plant to grow.

The availability of space: The space available significantly dictates the type of plant to grow in your system. Gliding plants naturally take up ample space to grow like pumpkins, melons. It will need you to get a larger area to be able to produce them with outstanding success. On the other side, small-sized plants like spinach, kale, etc. can be grown in every system when excellently tailor to fit them. These plants have a faster growth rate leading to harvests throughout the year.

Level of experience: Previous exposure to gardening, coupled with the reason for your investment in growing plants, can determine the choice of plant to grow. For starters, it is advisable first to cultivate simple and faster-maturing crops to feel the experience before venturing into complex to grow plants, especially the deep-rooted and vast plants. You will lose morale if you face challenges at the start. It is inevitable with sophisticated crops. However, with experience, you will be the one to inhibit using a hydroponic system because of countless benefits you will enjoy with the system.

The size of your water tank (reservoir): It is recommendable to use a water tank that is proportionate to the size of the plants grown. The proportionately ensures adequate water supply along with enough oxygenation to all the plants. In selecting the size of the reservoir to use, establish how much nutrient is needed by each plant walk back the calculation to determine the right size of the tank. Large plants like squash require much water meaning your reservoir will be bigger than for medium-sized plants such as herbs, peppers, etc. Smaller reservoirs create problems like withering of the plants, suffocation, and drowning due to insufficient oxygenation. Consequently, malnutrition and PH imbalance will set in affecting total plant health.

The selection of plants to grow using hydroponics

The following are some of the plants that grow well in hydroponic system if they are managed well.

Tomatoes: Tomatoes are one of the ideal plants that can thrive hydroponically. They belong to the family Solanaceae. Tomatoes can do well in both small space and extensive gardens. This makes it suitable for commercial and non-commercial growth. The ability to manage all the plant minerals and nutrients helps farmers cultivate and harvest tomatoes year in and year out continuously. Tomatoes harvested hydroponically do not lose their original taste as though they have grown organically in natural soil. Growers of this fruity plant benefit from getting a range of foods such as vitamins A, C, and antioxidants that cleanse the body and folic acid. However, it is essential to note that plants such as this require adequate lighting and hot temperatures. Tomatoes have week stems; this requires for them to be tied on to trellis or a pipe.

Lettuces: Lettuce belongs to the daisy family called Asteraceae, a leafy plant. Naturally, lettuce grows and matures faster, making it the most convenient choice of plant for growers. Like tomatoes, it allows for a continuous harvest throughout out enabling steady fresh supply. Growing lettuce is advantageous since it grows in a small space and any hydroponic system such as Deep Water Culture System, Drip System, and Wick System though the temperature must be kept cold. One can start to harvest lettuce in a matter of weeks, such a short period. The plant can be harvested continuously twelve weeks under a good climate condition, and it requires growing cold temperatures. Lettuce does not need a lot of light to grow. Lettuce contains vitamins A, C, and K and minerals like calcium, Potassium that boost human body metabolism.

Cucumber: Cucumber grows better in wet conditions, which makes them suitable for a hydroponic system. Cucumber is a source of sodium, zinc, magnesium, vitamin B, and C, including folic acid. These nutrients present in cucumber give it the ability to cleanse the body of fats and have anti-aging properties. However, growing cucumber requires sufficient space and total support because it is a crawling plant. But most all, the right proportion of its required nutrients must be supplied to the plant on time to increase its production.

Spring onions: Spring onions are usually harvested when the bulb has not yet swollen. Many onions can be planted in a single pot, and after every four weeks, they can be collected. These onions are rich in antioxidants, which protect human Deoxyribonucleic Acid (DNA) from being damaged and body tissues preventing somebody's actions. The presence of vitamins A, B, C, and K in onions boosts bones' health. These onions also have distinctive natural elements, which are importantly used in the treatment of infections that are caused by viruses. These health benefits of spring onions make it more marketable and a top choice for a hydroponic system.

Peppers: Peppers and tomatoes require the same conditions for growth. Though, it is recommended that room temperature has to be monitored and regulated all the time. The heat has to be reduced during the day and increased during the night if you need to maximize production. Peppers are known to raise appetite and flavour foods. Besides the presence of vitamins A and C, it is rich in fibre that seamlessly aids digestion.

Spinach: Spinach belongs to the family Spinacia oleracea. Like many other leafy vegetables, spinach does so well when planted using a hydroponic system. Spinach like lettuce can be harvested in a short period because of its ability to grow fast. The roots of this plant are immersed halfway into the nutrient solution. The nutrient solution is placed in a frame designed with a 5-inch depth. The hydroponic system uses technology that allows for complete control of plant growth by feeding the vital plant nutrients and minerals to the plants, including the regulation of environmental conditions like temperature and light. This provides suitable conditions that support the faster growth nature of this leafy plant. Lettuce is a good source of protein, vitamins, and rich with antioxidant minerals making this drop to be among the most beneficial vegetables health-wise. Spinach offers heart protection, reduces high cholesterol levels, and aids the digestion of food. The presence of copper, magnesium, zinc, iron, and folic acid, among others, makes spinach the most preferred vegetable for health reasons.

Strawberries: Strawberries are a popular fruit that belongs to the genus Fragaria. It is a hybrid species planted as a fruit. Strawberries are a common plant best for cultivation hydroponically. This fruit grows better in wet conditions and even has the best products in a hydroponic system. Consequently, strawberries yield better fruits when grown in a hydroponic system compared to when planted in soil. Strawberries in a hydroponic system can be harvested for a long time. The most common hydroponic system for growing strawberries is the Nutrient Film Technique, particularly for commercial cultivation.

It should be noted that weather is not necessarily a significant factor for strawberry growth hydroponically. Though it requires an abundance of light, which is natural, and exposure to sunlight, the warm temperature is ideal for growing strawberries. Like most fruits and vegetables, strawberries provide antioxidants to the body and vitamin C, which helps to strengthen immunity, thereby building high resistance to disease attacks. It also prevents blood pressure from building up by reducing cholesterols in the body.

Blueberries: They are categorized under cyan coccus, known to be a fruit with the most abundant antioxidants. Given that blueberries thrive in acidic conditions, the acidity of the water solution has to be equally acidic. However, it has to be monitored closely to avoid the acidity at the required level. The ability to control such conditions under a hydroponic system makes it suitable for growing blueberries. Regulation of soil pH is, therefore, the most crucial factor in growing blueberries. But thanks to hydroponics, monitoring of soil pH and level of nutrients has been made easy in this method of cultivation. The temperature must be maintained warm for better growth and yield. The most preferred and convenient hydroponic system for growing blueberries is the Nutrient Film Technique because blueberries require a transplant. Under the NFT system, transplanting is the best way to introduce the plants to the system. Its abundant antioxidants have unique properties that guard the brain as well as protecting the nervous system.

Basil: Basil belongs to the plant family Lamiaceae. Basil is known as another plant that can be grown with ease in a hydroponic system. Like blueberries, to grow basil, one needs to first get the seedlings either from their nursery bed or purchased externally from seedling growers. The seedlings then can be transferred to the hydroponic garden. But note that the soil on the seedling root has to be correctly and carefully cleaned by washing with water. Nutrient Film Technique and Drip System are the two hydroponic systems best suited for its growth. Once planted, ensure adequate lighting for more than eleven hours daily and regulate the temperature to warm. Insufficient light and hot or cold temperatures affect its production. As a herb, it is not surprising that basil has anti-inflammation properties, rich in antioxidants, which prevents free radicals from making humans from faster aging. Besides these health benefits, basil also gives an excellent taste to food with better aroma.

Coriander: Coriander is another herb that takes amazingly a shorter time to grow and can be harvested for about two or three times. It takes only four weeks to grow under favorable conditions. Unlike many other herbs, coriander does not need special attention though it requires an abundance of natural light to thrive and give higher harvest every time. Because coriander is a herb, it has significant health benefits such as prevention of skin inflammations, controlling high cholesterol level, ulcers of the mouth, helping in digestion to mention but a few. Food nutrients found in coriander include vitamins, protein, fiber, and magnesium.

Kale: Kale is very simple to grow, and the hydroponic system makes taking care of it much more manageable. It belongs to a class of cabbage called Brassica Oleracea. Kale, like spinach, is cultivated for its edible green leaves. This plant, preferably, can be cultivated using a hydroponic technique called Drip System, which farmers have used for ages. Kale thrives even when it is grown indoor. Pests less affect it. Therefore there is no need to stress about pesticides. The system temperature has to be regulated between warm and cold to increase its production.

Chives: Scientifically referred to as Allium Schoenoprasum, chives are consumable, which belong to species-genus Allium. Although chives are harvested after six months, they are still simple to grow hydroponically in favorable conditions. Once matured, there harvest period extends up to four weeks till when it is completely grown. To be able to harvest chives for up to three to four weeks or more, they must have access to sufficient natural sunlight for fourteen hours every day. Insufficient sunlight affects its growth and production. System temperature must be warm at all times.

Watercress: Watercress is a dark-like green that shares the same family Brassica Oleracea as kale. It is grown for its edible leaves. This plant naturally grows in a water running environment with its pungent leaves best as salads. This fact makes the hydroponic type of farming a better suite for growing watercress. Other plants such as blueberries require transplanting to the hydroponic system, but for watercress, the seeds are planted directly into the hydroponic pots meant for them. The pH of the mineral solution must be alkaline because this water-loving crop does well in a somewhat alkaline condition. Such requirement calls for total control and monitoring of the water solution alkalinity. The plant also requires a low temperature. Farmers may just plant this crop using its seeds, once, after which its stem can be chopped and fixed in another hydroponic pot for it to continue growing again because it can be planted using suckers like bananas.

Lotus: Lotus, also scientifically called Nelumbo Nucifera, is another water-loving crop. Immature lotus rhizomes are cut from the main mature root and placed correctly in hydroponic tubes; other people use pots. Lotus is grown on a bed of substrate like gravel. It is recommended to have a reservoir of water solution that is at least one foot tall. The best temperature for this water plant is warm, much as it can survive under relatively cold conditions. It is significant as always to research all the vital requirements of this plant before beginning to cultivate it or otherwise.

Radishes: Combined with other vegetables, radishes are a type of plant that adds great flavor to food. Radishes are per harps the most straightforward vegetable to grow in the soil-less condition, given the fact that they do not even require light like other plants to grow. It is advisable to start growing radishes from seeds, which will sprout between three to seven days. To have the best harvest, keep the system temperature cool, and continuously monitor the temperature. Regulate the solution pH between six and eight. Of course, the right nutrients in the right proportion must be fed to the crop.

Cultivating hard to grow plants using hydroponic technology

Many people think crops that are challenging and difficult to grow cannot be grown by the use of hydroponic technology. Yet, long time cultivators have repeatedly succeeded in growing plants in hydroponic systems and reaping a massive harvest they can't regret. Therefore, hard to cultivate plants require intensive care or would occupy considerable space when they grow.

Plants that require big space to grow: If you lack space, it is essential to avoid growing crawling plants such as pumpkins, melons, squash, and many other plants that take up significant space. Again this does not mean that these large plants cannot be grown hydroponically; it is only that obtaining a large plot of land to cultivate such crops will be expensive, and taking care of them in a small place is undoubtedly tricky. Subsequently, these plants will not thrive in squeezed areas compared to open large fields. Besides, it could prove to be uneconomical. For individuals who have a more significant chunk of land can well plant these crops easily and will succeed.

Deep-rooted vegetables: With hydroponic technology, the depth for plant root growth is not so deep inhibiting the growth of long-rooted vegetables, including plants with massive roots. It is a challenging factor for most hydroponic growers. Such crops are not advisable to be planted by growers who are yet new to this system of farming. They need first to acquire extensive experience to be able to manage long-rooted plants better. These plants include potatoes, turnips among many more others. A substrate is most required for such deep root tubers to support the high-depth roots adequately.

However, farmers with sufficient fields can customize it to suit deep-rooted tubers. If well set-up, bigger crops, root tubers, and other hard to grow plants can thrive in a hydroponic system as though they were planted in soil. Therefore, growth nutrient requirements for deep-rooted and hard to cultivate plants differ from natural simple and easy plants to grow. Importantly, it is best to understand the conditions favorable for the growth of the plant you have selected to grow.

CHAPTER THREE

The difference between gardening and hydroponics, The PROS and CONS of Hydroponics

Hydroponics and gardening

As discussed explicitly in the previous chapters, hydroponics involves the cultivation of various crops in a soil-less nutrient, and mineral-rich water solution mixed proportionately per the specific plant requirement. Unlike natural soil that already contains a blend of multiple nutrients vital for plant survival, hydroponic nutrients are extracted from various sources such as mineral salts, which is an equivalent of nutrients found in natural soil. The ultimate difference between nutrients in organic soil and hydroponic water solution is the rate of absorption of these minerals by plants as well as the speed of release of the nutrients. Considering this, the hydroponic system can result in the optimal production of food rich in nutrients within a shorter period.

Hydroponics has proved economically more viable in contrast to traditional soil-based gardening. It is so because the hydroponic system allows complete management and control of plant growth right from seeds to seedlings to a plant and finally to harvest time. Full control of plant elements like oxygen, carbon dioxide, light, and the temperature is significant for high-grade plant yield per harvest; this will maximize profits for growers. Each nutrient need for particular plants is studied and analyzed. The results of this analysis blend a set of requirements essential for the growth of these plants and are supplied directly to their roots in a water solution. The acidity and alkalinity of the water solution (pH) must be monitored as some plants only thrive in acidic conditions and others in alkaline conditions.

In a hydroponic setting, it has been investigated that, plants are less exposed to pests and diseases in comparison to plants cultivated in an open field. Generally, crops grown hydroponically are much healthier. It is this super health that builds their capacity to resist attack from disease; a sick crop placed right next to a healthy plant in a hydroponic system my not infect the healthy plant. This is simply because healthy plants are also highly resistant to fungal diseases due to their anti-fungal properties. Consequently, hydroponically grown plants save growers from the expense of buying pesticides and herbicides.

Traditionally cultivated crops tent to be more susceptible and prone to fungal infections as well as pests and diseases which require continuous spraying with pesticides and fungicides, yet eating chemically sprayed plants could have serious health repercussions on the consumer. Besides, the health complications that can come along with chemically sprayed plants, buying pesticides, herbicides, and fungicides can be expensive, thereby increasing the cost of production. Traditional gardening requires a big piece of land, meaning individuals without access to a plot of land may not be able to cultivate. Total exposure to natural calamities such as intense sunshine, flooding, strong winds among others can destroy plants grown traditionally.

Nutrients for hydroponic systems

Hydroponic technology has various methods of growing crops. The choice of selection precisely depends on the types of plants to grow, available space, and possible time to monitor and supervise the plants. In contrast, nutrients used in a hydroponic system are slightly different from those in organic soil as opposed to nutrients and minerals in a way that there are microelements designed explicitly for hydroponic systems; these microelements are paramount for plants. The hydroponic solution contains nutrients and minerals such as calcium, potassium, magnesium, manganese, copper, zinc, nitrogen, oxygen, boron, and many others fed to plant roots. Whereas dry and solid fertilizers are used in traditional gardening, hydroponic technology uses liquid fertilizer tailor-made for hydroponic growth; liquid fertilizers are slightly costly compared to dry and solid fertilizers.

The temperature of the water solution and oxygen for the roots
Hydroponic water solutions are not about basically blending the various plant nutrients and supply it to the roots, but rather it forms part of the root system zone. The root system zone is per harps more critical to plant survival than the outside environment. With plant minerals, the water solution also contains microscopic organisms without plants that may not survive as expected. Just like the plant and plant roots, these tiny organisms require favorable conditions for their survival; otherwise, they can perish and might perish along with the plants too. Therefore, the temperature and other elements of the water solution must be regulated to preserve these microscopic organisms.

The optimal or ideal water temperature should range from sixty-eight to seventy-two Fahrenheit. Given that this is a perfect temperature, temperatures slightly high or less can still be favorable. When water solution temperature drops far less or raises high, the plant will first start to deteriorate by weathering due to high temperatures in the root zone. Secondly, the microorganisms that kill plants because dangerous organisms like fungi can outmatch the organism that supports plant life, and bacteria survive best under warm temperatures. Using an aquarium water heater can raise cold temperatures. A hot temperature reduces water capacity to maintain the oxygen molecules present in the solution.

It should be noted that, just like human beings need oxygen for their survival, so do plants; otherwise, inadequate or absence of oxygen can suffocate plants to death. The hydroponic system that is likely to encounter such a problem is the Water Culture System involves partially immersing the roots into the solution. Therefore, temperature and the amount of oxygen in hydroponic nutrient water solution should be regulated and monitored closely to avoid complete loss of your crop farm.

Oxygen molecules lost due to hot temperatures can easily be replaced by installing an air pump right in the reservoir that contains the water solution. Smaller plants absorb a lesser amount of oxygen, and the opposite is exact with big plants. The presence of oxygen in the water solution lowers the chances of pathogen survival while it supports microorganisms to thrive, thereby boosting plant growth powerfully.

Artificial lighting for hydroponics
Crops can be grown hydroponically either by exposing them to natural sunlight or installing an artificial lighting system. To save yourself from additional expenses, it is better to utilize natural sunlight instead of hydroelectric power. The use of electric power can be inevitable if environmental conditions such as prolonged bad weather and inadequate space restrain access to natural lighting.

Types of artificial lighting
There are many varieties of artificial lighting systems available to pick from. Different plants have unique lighting needs, and this, therefore, necessitates careful selection. It ultimately means that the lighting system that works best for one plant may be the reverse for another. Artificial lighting systems include but not limited to.
- Fluorescent tube lights are known to be energy savers; fluorescent tubes do not heat light other lighting bulbs. It does not alter the temperature of the hydroponic system.

- T5 lighting fixtures, these come in numerous sizes. Understanding the needs of your plant and the growing space is essential in determining the correct lighting. The lighting fixture can hold one, two, four, six, or eight bulbs at the same time. The bulbs are about two or four feet long. So one should carefully choose to base on their needs. Two feet of tubes can fit in small areas, whereas four feet of bulbs fit in spacious areas.
- High-Intensity Discharge Lights (HID); this type of lighting system works using large bulbs, making it most convenient for larger spaces. It involves the ignition of the gas lit by the electric current that moves between electrodes near each other. HID are in two types, namely, High-Pressure Sodium and Metal Halide. To ensure continuous lighting of the hydroponic system, a steady flow of electric current must be maintained.
- Led lighting fixture, though rarely used in a hydroponic system, led lighting fixtures have existed for several years and are somewhat costly when compared to other lighting systems. However, it is crucial to remember that led lights may not deliver sufficient light to flowering plants. They may, therefore, not be ideal for floriculture.

Water solution PH regulators: The pH of the water solution is yet another vital aspect of the hydroponic system. PH regulators are simply machines used to restore acidity and alkalinity of the hydroponic water solution to the normal range. It is an excellent practice to maintain initial nutrients and other elements of hydroponic water solution other than introducing new things because it can mess up the pH. The quantity of pH regulator is determined by the size of your water solution and farm, but a pound of dry regulators may be used for up to six months to twenty-four months. Again, like temperatures and other minerals, specific plants survive better under different water solution pH conditions. PH regulators for liquids are not cheap, like dry PH regulators. That said, it is still important to purchase both up and down PH, do not think for a second that you require only one type. Otherwise, as humans, we are all liable to make mistakes. You may unintentionally raise the solution PH, yet you may not have down pH to lower it.

Pump timers: Because most hydroponic techniques are designed to function using water, water pumps were incorporated as part of the system to regulate the water level in the entire system. As a result, a 15-amp heavy-duty timer that can be used across the most hydroponic system is the right choice for growers who use it. Pump timers that have less than 15 amps are weak as they wear out faster in comparison to those with 15 amps. Cost-wise, 15-amp timers are cost-friendly, though this may depend on the store you bought. In waterlogged conditions, these grounded heavy-duty timers are recommended as they prevent shocks from electrical current.

Other timers include dial timers and digital timers. Digital timers would require more money to purchase compared to dial timers, also called mechanical timers. Digital timers can record and store past data regarding water level regulation. This function works on a battery system or can be connected to a source of power; otherwise, power blackout can wipe the entire system memory. Memory wipe is disadvantageous, as the timer may not automatically restart to work after power returns. Mechanical timers as cheap as they are will resume operating immediately when the power comes back hence avoiding memory loss.

Due to the variance in hydroponic systems and nature of the plants grown, there is equally a difference among all the various timers; they can be set up uniquely. Because of this fact, other pump timers are customized with limited pins within its dial. This improves its cycle options. Pump timers with a dial should be considered more than the ones without, most preferred is the fifteen-minute on and off minimally because of its versatility.

Water quality: Dirty water in itself is unclean. Filtered clean water enables efficient flow through the hydroponic tubes to each plant and eliminates the possibility of blocking the smaller tubes. The significance of fresh filtered water must never be overlooked in the hydroponic system you choose to use. This can have a significant impact on the health and quality of yields produced. Rain sources like wells, streams, taps, and rainwater can be problematic sometimes. Therefore, it is paramount to filter water from such sources. Although water cleaned by water softener purifies it well, it blocks or removes some valuable plant minerals as well. Meanwhile, toxic substances such as sodium chloride, a type of salt, can leak through the water softener and will accumulate in the water solution with time. Specific pathogens and spores of fungi are present in tap water as well as other many other chemicals. It acts as a breeding ground for various diseases, increases the solution toxicity, and creates significant variances in pH levels. Water from the well could have the most impurities. Though rich in microorganisms beneficial for plant growth, it harbours soil-borne sicknesses that are likely to transfer to your crops. Sturdy and robust plants can survive this toxin while others cannot.

To avoid all such stress and headache, just use clean water from the point go. Reverse Osmosis is the most suitable purification method for unclean water one can use. Apart from Reverse Osmosis, you can engineer your water purification system by use of simple filtration technology. Use multiple filters to ensure total filtration of impurities. The filtration filters include sediment, activated charcoal, and a micron filter. The quality of hydroponic water heavily depends on the filter quality used for the filtration. Once in a while, you are required to change and replace the filters.

The water level in your hydroponic system: Different types of hydroponic systems such as the NFT system, the Wick system, the Water Culture system, Drip system, among others, require a different amount of water. However, this also depends on the type of crop grown as well as the media in use. The difference in the water level requirement sets in because various growing mediums have unique water absorption and retention properties implying that media that can hold water longer will have stable water levels for a good time compared to those that have water retention capacity. Hydroponics' primary objective is to maintain crop roots wet except for the stems consistently; otherwise, they will decay.

Watering: Watering in a hydroponic system is influence by several factors like air and water temperature, media being used, and choice of the plant as well as space occupied by the plant. It should, however, be noted that watering in a hydroponic system is not the same as watering crops in traditional gardening. The ultimate objective of the hydroponic system is to grow plants either in water or in a moisturized environment. So the number of times to water in the hydroponic setting is not definite, but this could depend on the type of hydroponic system chosen and the area selected for growth; hotter and drier regions require frequent watering due to rapid water loss to evaporation. While cold environments do not need much irrigation, their roots must be kept wet.

Necessarily talking, water is most needed to keep plant roots wet and moist, enabling adequate absorption of plant nutrients introduced into the water solution. Small plants do not need a lot of water because they do not have many leaves compared to big ones. Likewise, crops in arid areas require enough water as opposed to the ones in humid regions. Growers need to be observant and keen on which hot and cold temperatures characterize months or seasons of the year; this simplifies planning ahead of time, thus avoiding surprises. Timely and scheduled watering maximizes crop production. However, oxygen in a hydroponic system circulates in the water solution; therefore, the water level should be allowed to drop far less. Otherwise, plants can suffocate in the event of insufficient oxygen absorption. If you are having challenges with your water level monitoring, you should consider installing pump timers.

Pros and Cons of hydroponic systems

Up to date, there are still considerable misconceptions about the advantages and disadvantages of adopting hydroponic technology as a system of agricultural farming. Much as traditional gardening has its benefits, they do not surpass the gains a grower can get from using a hydroponic system. Let us start by exploring the pros of the hydroponics system as below.

Pros of hydroponic system

Free from chemicals: Hydroponically cultivated crops are not much exposed to pests and diseases. Soil offers favourable breeding grounds for many soil-borne diseases, side-lining the use of soil, thus preventing such diseases from attacking your crops. Healthy plants build high resistance to pests and diseases, reducing the use of pesticides, among other chemicals. Plants that are less sprayed with compounds potentially have more robust yields with better nutritional value.

Space minimization: Hydroponic cultivation is known for space utilization in contrast to traditional methods of farming. Traditional gardening works on the principle that plant roots need bigger space in search for water and other nutrients and minerals. However, this has entirely been replaced by a hydroponic system whereby roots are either fully or partially immersed in an oxygen-rich water solution. Above all, plant growth is holistically regulated and monitored in hydroponics. Plants are confined in small containers or canes to save space. Besides, a plant grown in a hydroponic system grows faster as a mixture of balanced nutrients, and plant minerals foster growth. This leaves space to grow the next plant. It is a vertical method of growing plants in hydroponics that saves a significant amount of space compared to traditional gardening.

Set and forget control: Except for traditional farming, hydroponic technology grants you full control of your plant's life and the kind of products you want to harvest. Factors that affect plant growth, such as nutrient availability, lighting, air, and water temperature, including humidity, can be fully managed in a hydroponic setting. Taking into account the various requirements of individual plants, you can develop an effective combination of plant nutrients, the ideal temperature, exposure to light, amount of oxygen, to mention but a few. Here you are solely in charge of your plant's well-being.

Water conservation: It is almost impracticable to cultivate in desert areas using traditional farming. It is easy and simple to cultivate in those areas using hydroponic technology due to the water-saving ability of the system. The difference here is that hydroponic systems can recycle the water they use, and this water is kept in a water tank that is then controlled. Besides, the quantity of water required to irrigate crops in traditional farming for a single day may be used for about a week in hydroponic technology.

No digging and weeding involved: Plants in hydroponics can grow right in your veranda, rooftop, or inside a room (indoor) provided there is access to either natural light or artificially tailored lights for the system. This eliminates the tiresome work of preparing the cultivation field and weeding as they grow. Cultivating soil is provoking as it takes too much time, depending on the size of the area. The hydroponic system only takes a bucket and nutrient water solution to feed the plants.

Scientology: The hydroponic system uses scientific technology to grow plants. Through such technology, growers get to comprehend better the nutrient demands of their plants as well as the best environment that support their growth. Better still, you can also design your system that fits in the available space you have, controlling water PH and temperature. Therefore, hydroponics allows for full customization of the entire growth processes and procedures after studying the reactions of every plant to these conditions, such as what is the response of lettuce to high or low temperatures or what solution PH is best for spinach. You will undoubtedly enjoy healthy, high yields if you understand these various needs and properties of these plants.

Easy to grow locally: Due to the simplicity with which plants can grow hydroponically, it is likely to even cultivate them in the smallest space you have in your backyard. The possibility of everyone growing their food even in an urbanized location solves the global challenges of food shortages. Food prices could fall considerably if people produced hydroponically.

Aids soil conservation: Hydroponic growing principally uses no soil at all. But instead, a mixture blended with plant nutrients is supplied to the plants to grow. While growers cultivate using hydroponic technology, the traditional farmlands keep fallowing, thereby restoring their fertility for some time. Growth mediums that are particularly impartial are wielded to hold up plant roots, including its overall weight. Media growers apply in hydroponic are, in most cases, permeable with the potentiality to allow water to pass in the event of absorption by plant roots and have the capability to keep oxygen for the plants.

High efficiency: After successfully replace the soil with a water solution, it was recorded that plant growth propagation increased by at least two times for most crops. The plant growth rate increased because crop roots redirect much of the energy they would have wielded to pierce soil in look for nutrients and minerals to foster their growth. Expectedly, this will remarkably amplify higher production. Faster plant growth is profoundly uplifted due to the presence of all the nutrients and minerals, including the availability of oxygen noteworthy for their growth.

Minimal exposure to pests and diseases: Essentially, the absence of soil means substantially abolishing breeding ground and the manifestation of pests and diseases. Presence of soil aids the prevalence of pests and other diseases. Wholly substituting land as a growing media with water solution enables getting rid of potential pest and disease outbreak. However, pests and diseases are known to inhibit rapid, thereby leading to stunted growth. As a result of this, several growers have resorted to eliminating pests and diseases by spraying chemicals, especially pesticides, and herbicides. But again, agricultural researchers have investigated that chemically sprayed plants are liable to yielding less nutritious produce, which makes them less marketable compared to hydroponically produced yields. Besides, apart from being hazardous to the environment, chemicals are not that cheap to afford. This raises the cost of production, which hikes the price for final products in the market. In general, hydroponics elevates healthy living.

Promotes total growth of plants: Plants can utilize their growth potential wholly in a hydroponic system. Plants can readily access nutrients and minerals made available to them in the water solution kept in a reservoir. Plants can consequently focus on their growth, thus achieving better health. It is aided by a faster absorption rate, as nutrients are just right in the solution where the roots lie.

Conservation and sustainability: Per harps sustainability and conservation of resources makes a more substantial portion of the hydroponic system. The practice in the hydroponic system is that water in the reservoir is reusable by recirculation it tall over again in the hydroponic system. The same water after recirculation can be transferred for use in other traditional gardens. The decontamination technology in hydroponics provides a mechanism for disinfecting the gray water, thereby recycling it. Other materials such as grow stones that operate as perfect solution absorbent and promoting efficient air circulation in the system can all be used over again.

No soil required: The capacity to cultivate crops just in water without using soil as a growing medium extends farming in "wastelands" or extremely contaminated arable land of the world. Locations that have only poor soils with desert climate can now utilize hydroponic technology to timelessly harvest crops in those areas. Fresh, nutritious foods have become available even in hard to cultivate areas like some parts of Israel. Hydroponics is, therefore, on a global scale, uplifting societies that could not reach fresh foods to enjoy one. Additionally, astronauts, while mostly dependent on food grown hydroponically as plant life, cannot be supported in space.

Climate control: The same way people have complete management of climatic conditions like a light for photosynthesis, components of air, and heat levels in a greenhouse is precisely how these conditions are controlled in the hydroponic setting. Growing plants year in and year out is possible in hydroponics since external environmental factors do not affect the plant's ability to grow and thrive. Growers can, therefore, sell produce throughout every season.

Effective use of nutrients: Growing plants hydroponically starts by identifying which plant to grow and what is that vital nutrient it needs to thrive. Once these nutrients or minerals are carefully defined, they are blended into one water solution. It is proved that this makes the plants grow faster than average.

PH control: Water PH has an extreme impact on the rate of nutrient absorption by roots. Mixing all nutrients in one solution gives the grower the ability to correctly measure the PH level and regulate them within the normal range.

Cons of hydroponics

Hydroponics requires time and commitment: The hydroponic system demands close attention and commitment to maximize production. In traditional gardening, plants can survive for a long time, yet hydroponics calls for close monitoring and supervision. Given that hydroponic plants survive on a mixture of nutrients fed to their roots by a person and regulation of essential components like water PH and temperature, they can hardly produce healthier produce when left unattended. Besides, hydroponic systems need maintenance such as replacing its parts like blocked small tubes, faulty pumps, and timers as well as cleaning the system, including water in the reservoir. Here plant's survival entirely relies on your commitment.

Expertise and technical know-how: Hydroponic systems function by operating multiple modes concurrently, yet they all require unique special skills. Additionally, knowing the kind of plant to grow and determining their unique surviving properties in hydroponic setting all call for technical knowledge. Otherwise, a slight error in setting up the system can doom your entire farm.

Organic debates: Globally, there are differences in opinion as to whether hydroponically grown plants satisfy all the requirements for organic certification. Soil contains microbiomes that are naturally absent in hydroponic water solutions, which are essential for plants. To solve the problem of the absence of microbiomes, growers have resorted to the incorporation of natural minerals such as alfalfa and bones, among others.

Risk of electricity shock: Hydroponic technology functions with the use of water and electricity. Usage of electricity exposes people to the risk of suffering power shock in close range. It is, therefore, advisable to wear protective gear that is non-conductor of electricity.

Risk of system failure: Like any mechanical system, the hydroponic system relies on electricity or at least some form of a power source. The danger here is that the entire system can be shut down should there be a power blackout. When every system is halted, water and oxygen circulation will stop, and the plants will begin to shrink with immediate effect. If the power blackout extends for hours, the plants can dry out. You need to have a severe contingency power plan to prevent a total loss. Remarkable, this affects large-scale growers and not small-scale growers.

Start-up cost: Technology such as this does not come cheaply. The initial set-up cost is enormous because you will need to buy a range of types of equipment like a reservoir, minerals, lighting system, and a timer, among others. However, this cost will eventually come down after initial installations. You may only continue to incur maintenance costs, which is not that substantial.

Returns take a long period to realize: To reap big in a hydroponic system, one needs to cultivate on a large-scale. Yet large-scale investments require colossal amounts of money. Enormous amounts of cash, like in any other investments, take a long time to recover it. Unless an investor has required the initial capital investment, they cannot say they are making provides. A carefully planned and thought out business plan can foretell when you can begin to realize profits.

The quick spread of pests and diseases: Plants are nearly spaced to each other in hydroponic systems. In the event of disease manifestation, all plants in that system can be affected and catch the disease. The rapid spread of pests and disease is catalysed by the fact that plants share the same source of nutrients and water. Therefore, large-scale hydroponic growers must have a detailed strategic disease prevalence management structure. Otherwise, the whole hydroponic farm can be doomed in a matter of hours or days.

Consequently, the benefits associated with hydroponic technology outstandingly outweigh the advantages of traditional gardening. The significance of the hydroponics system ranges from remarkably increasing total crop production to environmental conservational and many others in between. Traditional gardening can never be compared to a hydroponic system of farming. With an influx of many manufacturers investing hugely in producing hydroponically used equipment, the potential possibility to overtake traditional gardening shortly is progressively higher.

CHAPTER FOUR

Hydroponic System, Types of hydroponics systems (Pros and Cons of each system)

Hydroponic system

Scientists and agriculturalists have worked tirelessly in a bid to invent and discover soil-less means of cultivation. Well, their attempt was successful; they found hydroponic technology for farming. Unlike traditional gardening, hydroponics replaces soil with a water solution that contains all essential plant nutrients and minerals vital for plant survival. Plant roots are placed directly into the nutrient solution that contains oxygen, which is absorbed by the plant. As discussed in the previous chapter, one of the advantages of a hydroponic system is that it fosters fast plant growth primarily because of the availability of plant nutrients and other elements of plant growth such as light and regulated temperature to favorable levels. However, you many blend the right proportions of nutrients required by a particular plant, but if you do not monitor temperature, humidity, solution PH, and access to either natural sunlight or artificially manufacture light needed for photosynthesis, the plants will never thrive. You can never have the best harvest until you fix correct this problem.

You can consult a specialist before you indulge in the hydroponic system of farming because there are some hydroponic systems from which you can choose. Installing and setting up each system is unique. The choice of which method to use depends on some factors we shall discuss later in this chapter.

The main six types of hydroponic system
Hydroponic technology has several farming systems though most of them are simply a modification and integration of the main six types of hydroponic systems. Below are the specific types of hydroponic systems, including their respective advantages and disadvantages, for you to make a proper choice.

Deep-water culture system: Deep-water culture, as one of the hydroponic systems, entails freezing, hanging, or suspending plants in water that is sufficiently aerated. Also referred to as the DWC method, it is the most straightforward and universal system of hydroponic technology the market has witnessed. The method wields oscillated net pots containing crops above a deep-water tank supplied with oxygenated water, in which plant nutrients dissolve. Crop roots are therefore swamped in the water, enabling direct access to minerals, oxygen, and other components present in the nutrient solution. Many individuals have looked at the Deep-water system to be the most genuine type of hydroponic system. Because the entire plant root system is engulfed in water twenty-four hours a day, it accesses sufficient oxygen crucial for plants to thrive. Insufficient oxygen for the plants consequently suffocates them to death. The most typical solution to this problem is to use air stone linked directed to the pump that pushes oxygen from down the water tank to the whole hydroponic system. This air stone is also vital in air circulation.
It's convenient and straightforward to install and set-up anywhere because the deep-water system does not require costly hydroponic

components and works in limited space like in your backyard. A small-uncontaminated bucket is suitable to keep the water solution and float a material on it to harbour the pot containing the nutrient source. Do not entirely swamp the plant, not even the stock into the answer but only the roots.

Advantages of Deep-water culture system

Deep-water culture hydroponic system is not a popular choice for nothing. It has benefits for its use as a method. Firstly, it has an insignificant maintenance cost. Once installed and fully set-up, maintenance is easy. What you need to do is only to refill the water solution should the level drop below the required and monitor oxygen supply to the plant roots, so keep the pump working all the time. Otherwise, it shutdown will cut the oxygen supply to the plants. Even refilling the solution is not a daily job because it can be done after about two weeks, but note that how big or small your crops hugely determine this are. Abundant crops will demand frequent replenishment of the nutrient solution, and small ones require the very opposite.

Secondly, anyone can be able to design his or her Deep-water culture system at the comfort of his or her home. You only need to have an air pump, nutrients, and minerals needed as well as the seedlings to plant.

Disadvantages of Deep-water culture system

Although a deep-water culture system is the most preferred system of hydroponic technology by small-scale farmers, it has some setbacks of using it. Firstly, the deep-water system is fantastic only for quick-growing plants such as lettuce and not best for slower growing and flowering plants. However, given additional intensive care, vegetables such as tomatoes and peppers, among others, can thrive in this system.

Secondly, it is most desired that the temperature of your system should not pass sixty-eight Fahrenheit and drop lower than sixty Fahrenheit. Unlike another system where the water solution keeps recirculation, with a Deep-water system, the water solution is quite static, making it a little challenging to regulate its temperature. Your plant life and total output are compromised if you cannot control the temperature levels.

Wick systems: Wick system involves placing your crops on a tray-like structure put above the water tank. The crops are cuddled in the growing medium. The water tank harbours the water solution in which all required plant nutrients are intermixed. Employing capillarity, water solution travels through to tray in which the plants ultimately grow. The mixed plant nutrients in the solution run up the wicks and circulate through the growing plant, enabling easy absorption of nutrients by the plant roots which they utilize for their growth. Local materials like rope and string can simply make the wicks. Though the deep-water system is easy to make, the wick system is the easiest method of hydroponic systems. It is a system that does not even necessitate mechanical automation of the components such as timers or pumps to operate. Therefore, it is best suited for locations where access to hydropower has remained a myth or unreliable.

Wick method operates through the process of capillarity, enabling uptake of the water solution in which the plants are submerged. The porous material utilized that transmits the water solution aids water absorption. The absence of transmittance makes the wick system non-functional, as the nutrient solution will not be forwarded to the plant roots. Cocoa coir obtained from coconut is the most convenient as its porous property increases its ability to hold moisture for a considerable time and non-combatant to water PH. It has no impact on solution PH. It is imperative to note that in contrast to other systems, a wick system operates with no speed inhibiting the choice of plant to grow in this system. This calls for individualizing the wick system from the solution water tank to every plant in the system. The necessity of keeping the wicks near to the root environment is crucial.

Advantages of the wick system

Wick system of hydroponics offers some benefits to the grower, such as; simplicity in terms of installation and assembling. The system is not too technical, so anybody can just set it up and does not need much commitment once it is up and functioning. Fast-growing plants like lettuce can thrive just fine given the consistent flow of water and nutrients to the crops hence eliminating the possibility of burning out.

Another advantage of the system is that it can fit in the smallest areas you have, whether a balcony or a veranda. This qualifies any location for this method of hydroponics. It is most recommended for starters, though.

Disadvantages of a wick system

Much as the wick system is the simplest method of hydroponics, it does not make it a challenge and setback free, which includes but not limited to; grower hindrance to growing only fast-maturing plants like lettuce. In this system, cultivators cannot plant vegetables like tomatoes, carrots, or even herbs because they demand vast water, which is not the case in a wick system setting. This limits the choice of plants to cultivate using this system to quickly maturing plants. If a grower grows crops that require much water in a wick system, they will likely die or not produce the expected output. Secondly, plants in this system are prone to decomposition due to dampness. It can cause fungal and bacterial infections, which impacts on total crop output.

Nutrient film technique system (NFT): Nutrient film technique hangs crops on the top of consistently flowing mineral solutions that runs forth and back the plant root system. The tributaries catching the plant are held in a position lowered down at one end, ensuring a seamless run of the nutrient solution up to the system tray before it reaches the water tank. The water in all hydroponic systems is aerated using air stone, meaning the NFT system is not an exception. The nutrient is pushed to the reservoir and back up with the help of a water pump. The system re-circulates the water, thereby reusing over and again except other systems where plant roots are immersed in the solution. In the NFT system, water runs to their ends, the extreme root points will splash the moisture to where the crops are, and as for the roots, they are supplied with enough oxygen. The ends of the trough are in a way that the shallow coat moves above the root tip, swiftly controlling wetting the system environment. Much as the Nutrient fill technique is known for recycling the water, it is essential to empty the water tank and refill the nutrients periodically. The gradient of the slope through which the water flows should never be so steep to prevent the speedy flow of nutrients. Plants will not adequately absorb the nutrients should the slope be too steep. It should be a gentle sloping. NFT system has gained much traction among commercial growers because numerous plants can be set up in a single trough leading massive production. Be cautious about heavy and large plants as the NFT system correctly supports simple plants with simple weight like spinach, strawberries, and kale. But with the help of trellis, vegetables like tomatoes can be grown using NFT, and the trellis supports the system.

Advantages of the NFT system

The recirculation ability of the nutrient film technique prevents wastage of resources, particularly water and nutrients. The continuous running water eliminates the salt minerals in the trough and around the root system. A nutrient film technique eliminates the use of a growing media, which saves the cost of purchasing them.

Nutrient film technique encourages production on large-scale this makes it perfect for commercialized growing. A single operating channel can easily be enlarged to incorporate more plants into the system. But it is essential to design a separate water tank for each channel. Additionally, in the case of pump breakdown, the prevalence of diseases cannot circulate to the rest of the system.

Disadvantages of NFT system

The critical failure of the NFT pumping system means the solution with its nutrients cannot circulate, thereby drowning the plants and consequently drying. Plants in this system are so delicate that they will be doomed in a few hours. You have to be very alert when using this system. Ensure continuous monitoring and supervision of the system, focusing more on the pump area.

The fact that different plants can be grown in one channel promoting the congestion of the plants. Crowding of plants has an impact on their root system. The roots will become closely spaced, creating competition for oxygen and food nutrients, resulting in starvation and malnutrition. You can decongest the system by uprooting some of the plants in the crowded zones.

Ebb and Flow system: In the Ebb and flow system, a bed specially prepared to grow plants is placed above a reservoir filled with nutrients over which the grow bed is put. A timer is fitted on the water pump placed in the tank. The pump will automatically begin to supply water to the grow bed after switching on the pump timer. Stopping the timer swiftly empties the grow bed by gravitational process recycling it back to the reservoir. Because of the possibility of flooding associated with the system, a tube is attached to the system to control the expected flooding. The plants will utilize the nutrients by extending their roots into the solution right below the grow bed. The grow bed is flooded in a specific interval to allow the plant root system to get enough oxygen before the subsequent flooding.

The Ebb and flow system is a standard system because of fostering plant growth vigorously and healthy harvests due to the availability of required plant nutrients fed to the plant roots. The flexibility and customization feature of the system allows for the growth of numerous pants like vegetables and herbs at the same time. Ebb and Flow system provides for the growth of most vegetables. If not all, the only inhibition is how deep and wide your tray is. Tubers need more deep grow beds as opposed to small rooted plants like strawberries. Grow rocks, extended pebbles, among others, are some alternative media you can select to use. Such grow media can be used repeatedly; it is not heavy yet has massive water retention capability, which is an essential property in Ebb and flow system.

Advantages of Ebb and Flow System
The advantages of using this method of the hydroponic system include firstly Ebb, and flow system, which permits total flexibility as growing big

plants, is possible as opposed to a deep-water culture system. Most plants like vegetables, herbs as well as flowering plants react positively to this form of hydroponic technology; as a result, plants highly thrive in this system.

Besides, there are various ways one can build their own Ebb and flow system locally at the comfort of their home. Due to its versatility, Ebb and flow systems are known to relatively sustain the most plant life compared to other systems.

Disadvantages of Ebb and Flow system
Like the Nutrient Film Technique, this system is likely to suffer occasional pump failure. When the pumping system shuts down, the possibility that your crops will all die is a guarantee. Again close supervision and periodically checking the system for faults is vital to identify and fix them. Water flow speed has to be moderate to allow adequate absorption of plant nutrients, thereby aiding healthy growth.

The possibility of plant decay and the manifestation of diseases is present if the cleanliness of the grow bed is not ensured. It arises out of poorly drained grow bed. Furthermore, many crops may not react positively to the ever-changing PH of the water solution caused by periodically draining and refilling the grow bed with nutrients

Drip system: Like other hydroponic systems, the drip system also uses aerated water containing nutrients, which a pump pushes through a series of tubes leading to every single plant in the system. Bit-by-bit, the nutrient solution drips unhurriedly into the plant media within the root environment maintaining the moist condition of the roots. Like the Ebb and flow system, a Drip system is widely used among large-scale growers. The system ranges from single crops to enormous irrigation activities. Drip systems may be configured in two different ways, such as recovery and non-recovery. The recovery configuration works on the principle that abundant water is emptied from the grow bed and re-circulated back to the reservoir at various intervals until the next phase. Whereas, when it comes to non-recovery configuration, the abundant water outflows from the grow bed and cannot be reused but passed out as wastage. The recovery system best works for home farmers while non-recovery interests' large-scale farmers. As wasteful as it seems, large-scale farmers use water perpetually. This even makes them more conservative when it comes to water use. The absolute difference between this system and its counterparts it that it is crafted to supply the exact amount of water needed to wet the area within the plant. Continuous recirculation of water in this system authorizes variations in the solution PH. The grower has to be alert to regulate the PH level at all times properly.

Advantages of Drip system

The drip system permits the growth of considerable plants in the system. Per harps, this is solely why large-scale growers most prefer it. Plants that consume ample space like pumpkins melons to mention, but a few can be sustained in this form of hydroponics. It can also support more growing medium like coco coir peat moss etc. giving it the capacity to bear large roots.

A drip system can uphold the commercialization of your small-scale production. Precisely, Drip system seconds the addition of more plants to the existing system by merely interconnecting new tubes as well as the installation of more reservoirs to support the new nutrient and water capacity.

Disadvantages of Drip System

Despite the tremendous significance of this system, it still has some challenges, such as maintaining the required PH level, continually emptying and refilling the water, and controlling the nutrient amount for the non-recovery system. That said, large-scale growers suffer from blockage caused by pilling of dirt and salt along the tube. This compromises the delivery of nutrients to the plant roots, thereby affecting their growth and total output. Frequent cleaning is highly required.

The drip system though, can be easily customized; it is more sophisticated for growers. This proves it to be less recommended for small-scale home cultivators as it requires more specialized skills for effective operation. Other hydroponic systems like the Ebb and Flow system have proven to be more favorable for home growing.

Aeroponics: Except in other systems, Aeroponic systems tend to be unique. In this system, the bare plant roots system is hanged in the air with nutrients sprayed in the form of constant mist. Depending on individual preferences, one can select cubes or a tower-like structure to contain several plants in a single tower bound by frames. Like the rest of the systems, the nutrient solution is kept securely in a reservoir, which by using the water pump, the nutrient is snouted, and it eventually evenly spreads like a mist. The upper part of the tower drops the fog that settles down the chamber, reaching the plants. The mist consistently descends directly on to the plant roots allowing them to absorb the vital growth nutrients. Substrate media is not required in the Aeroponic system to sustain plant life. The mist contains abundant oxygen because the system is open to the air, which rapidly increases its growth.

Because of the conversion of water solution to mist, the Aeroponic system uses water more conservatively than its counterparts. Again compared to others, it only uses five percent of the water that other systems use. The Aeroponic system tower is projected upwards, thereby economizing space to establish more towers in the same place. The sufficient delivery of oxygenated mist quickens plant growth allowing constant growth throughout the entire year. Vegetables such as tomatoes, eggplants, and leafy plants like lettuce, including others like strawberries, herbs, and ginger all thrive in the Aeroponic system. However, note that plants that flourish below the ground like carrots, cassava, and fruity plants cannot fit in the Aeroponic method because they are heavy and large.

Advantages of Aeroponic system
The abundantly available source of oxygen accelerates plants' maturity. Apart from being the best hydroponic system in terms of productivity, they are environmentally friendly, how amazing. Besides, the hydroponic

system is known for its flexibility and the ability to tailor its individual plant needs, thus maximizing production.

Aeroponic systems can seamlessly be shifted from one site to the others due to the ease with which they transport. The tray and the tower are lightly weighted, making it convenient to move them without interrupting the plants. Coherently, you need to spray the mist with your hands to prevent the crops from withering and dry out. Utilizing space is another advantage of the hydroponic system due to the vertical projection of the tower that can hold many plants simultaneously.

Disadvantages of Aeroponic system

Cost-wise, the Aeroponic system can be unaffordable due to the high initial installation and assembling cost. Components such as water tanks, timers, etc. must be acquired before you operational this system. It is recommended for small-scalars to construct their hydroponic system locally to avoid unnecessary costs. It is a fixed cost for large-scalars to incur.

Aeroponics system also keeps a fragile balance, which can be dangerous in the event of any interruption. Malfunction of the water pump can doom the whole farm unless you spray the mist by yourself; otherwise, the entire system will dry out. Disinfecting and cleaning the chambers should frequently be to atop the risk of disease manifestation and accumulation of salt. Consequently, this builds up the maintenance cost for the system.

Other various combinations of hydroponic systems

As aforementioned, the central six hydroponic systems can be merged to create a new one. Hydroponic systems can be united to form several other methods, which can be unique from the parent systems. The most popular combined methods include.

The Krafty system: Integrating Water Culture System with Wick System results in a non-circulatory system referred to as Kraft System. A net pot like in the parent system is used for inserting a growing media and plants through a cut to fix the cup. The root system can formerly be swamped in the nutrient water with an air space to allow oxygen supply to the plants. The plants will quickly begin to grow as the roots consume the nutrients through the media. The lower the water level, the higher the oxygen concentration due to the more open-air spaces. Therefore, this permits maximum oxygenation of the plant necessary for their growth. The benefits of this method include total affordability, require minimum maintenance, and suitable for starters. Like any other method, the kraft system also has disadvantages such as; most practical for small-scale growers only and can only accommodate non-leafy plants limiting its usage for leafy plants like lettuce.

Dutch Bucket System: The modification of the Ebb and Flow System to wield one bucked where plant nutrient is delivered merely from the top through an outflow pipe lying under connecting to the water tank. Unlike the Krafty system, the Dutch Bucket System is usable for large-scale growers due to the possibility of interconnecting a separate irrigation system to the main. Transportation and transfer of the plants are quite easy because each bucket only contains an individual plant.

In the Dutch Bucket System, a media with high moisture retention capacity is most advisable with enough aeration. The perfect drainage system should be installed to eliminate blockage of the tubes while re-circulating the water solution. However, the pump in this system is only used to deliver the mineral solution to the interlinked separate buckets at the top. System maintenance must be frequently done together with monitoring salt and water solution PH to ensure balance. Do not plant seeds directly in the buckets but instead use a Rockwool. After germination, you can transplant the seed in the buckets. The best growing media for this system includes vermiculite, and coconut coir, on the other hand, should not be used in this system because of its gradual absorption property. If you insist on using coconut coir, then the non-recovery method is the best as the water will not re-circulate and accumulate, and the bit-by-bit emptying system must be used.

Dutch Bucket System is beneficial for supporting commercial growth, significant water conservation, and fostering plant growth, increasing the number of harvest year-round. Despite these advantages, this hydroponic has few challenges, such as requiring high-quality components to guarantee success, and the maintenances cost is relatively high.

Fogponics: The fogponics came as a result of modifying the Aeroponic system of hydroponics to better plant growth. Installation of a fog-creating component is incorporated into the system, which substitutes spraying mist periodically. The fogger maintains the humidity of the plant's surroundings. The water droplet in the system is tremendously resized to smaller droplets aiding perfect nutrient supply that sparks hairy root growth expanding root surface.

The pros of this modified Aeroponic system include; conservation of water and nutrient spoilage remarkably, absence of recycling prevents dilution of the solution, thus maintaining solution PH, and lastly, the system is straightforward to assemble. Dutch Bucket System also has a number of cons, including; trapping the mist to avoid starvation and drying of the plants, high start-up costs, frequently cleansing the system requires commitment as well as electricity blackouts can make the plants perish causing severe losses.

Components of the hydroponic system

Some hydroponic growers don't reap the most benefits out of the hydroponic system. They are not familiar with the principal operations of hydroponics. They don't realize how crucial it can prove to be if you do not familiarise yourself and comprehend the components of hydroponics. Let us look at some of the available parts of hydroponic that could lead to your success.

The growing media: Hydroponically, an immovable media is made use of to grow crops, which holds their overall weight and harbours its root system. The media alternatively replaced soil and required plant nutrients are delivered to the plant root system through the media, which retains the moisture. A lot of the growing media are designed to be non-combatant to solution PH, avoiding the interference with PH level.

Honestly speaking, the type of growing media used highly depends on the kind of plant you intend to grow, and the hydroponic system chosen. All the varieties of growing media are readily available in most agricultural stores and can be purchased via the Internet.

Air stones and pumps: Plants in the hydroponic system are most likely to drawn if not aerated. Immersing air stones helps to displace small air vacuums, which is supplied to the plants as oxygen after dissolving. The air vacuum dispenses the nutrient solution evenly to the plants. You have to note that the air stones do not produce oxygen in a hydroponic system, but rather a connected air pump helps to suck the air from outside into the reservoir through an opaque substance.

Netted pots: Hydroponics requires the use of pots in which the plants are placed and held as they grow. The pots are designed with holes that permit the roots to extend out in search of nutrients and access enough oxygenation. The netted pot allows better emptying of the solution as opposed to other pots.

Determinants of hydroponic systems

The types of hydroponic systems have been explicitly exhausted above. But the real question is, do you know which system works for you? Ok. Analyzing the functions and your hydroponic requirements would be a good start for you. To answer this critical question about your choice of hydroponic system, let us look at the factors you could consider.

Start-up cost: Not every hydroponic system will be affordable for you. Your budget can consequently determine whether you will invest in a small scale or large scale. The small size is desirous for small budgets, and it has faster returned on investment, while commercial growth is quite expensive, and the rate of return on investment takes a long time.

Availability of time: Most of the hydroponic systems demand a lot of attention, such as monitoring and supervision. Although plant growth to maturity may require less of your input apart from regulating the PH and control solution temperature, you have to create time to activities like disinfecting the equipment, transferring the plants to the growing pots and beds, harvesting, trimming among others. That said, usually, plants require even closer attention in the few days or weeks of planting. It is beneficial for you to begin small and expand in the future to get used to the tedious work involved. So if you certainly will not create time for your hydroponic system, then you better not dare to invest in it.

All in all, the Hydroponic system remains the best type of farming method despite some few challenges and setbacks it has. There are many types of hydroponic systems, both the significant types and integrated types. The overall success of every system is determined by carefully analyzing various plant requirements vital for their survival, feeding it to the plants on time, and controlling other environmental aspects such as humidity, temperature, and light. Ultimately the type of hydroponic system to use is dependant on the choice of plant, availability of space, time, and level of expertise.

CHAPTER FIVE

How hydroponic systems are built, various steps, Possible Problems

How hydroponic systems are built

Hydroponic systems are incredibly designed to utilize the soil-less medium for plant growth. As we all now, hydroponic technology employs the use of a water solution in which vital plant nutrients are dissolved and supplied with oxygen critical for plant sustainability. There are various hydroponic systems, some of which are integrated and modified but can all be tailored to your specific needs. It makes it somewhat simpler to create your hydroponic system locally. The information below relates to how you can build a hydroponics system at home for small scale growing or large scale growing.

A simple Wicked System: By using a pair of scissors, get an empty bottle and cut it off entirely about 10 cm measured from its top. Each empty bottle will contain only one plant. So if you need to grow many plants at the same time, instead of a small container, you get a 20 USAID gallon.

Drive a sharp object through the bottle top to create a hole. Place it on a stiff board-like surface to create the hole swiftly without a struggle. The gap should have a width of approximately 0.64 cm. You can make up to four holes.
Twist a piece of the strong thread via the hole. The string of thread lengthwise should be about 30cm long. Upon fixing the thread through the hole, ensure a balance on both sides of the bottle to 15 cm each. After passing the thread through, tie it to the container. More substantial water tanks may require a bigger rope to transfer abundant water to the system.

At this point, you can create a blend of nutrients by intermixing the various nutrients determined by your plant's choice. Place the already mixed nutrient solution in the bottle, and the container should measure about 950 ml of water. If you already purchased a mixed nutrient solution, follow the instruction menu stuck on the bottle to help you drop in your solution. Do not use hard water, but rather disinfected water is preferred.

Turn the bottle upside down as you put it to immerse the twisted thread or string in the solution. The total distance between the bottle head and the solution top should be approximately 2.5 cm for easy absorption of the nutrient by the media. If you used a plastic container, about 10.2 cm make holes align with the ones in the plastic tote.

Find suitable media that can permit swift movement of the nutrient solution to the plant roots like vermiculite or perlite, among others. Depending on the size of your bottle, evenly sprinkle the solution media on top of the bottle pressing it loosely. Here can proceed to transplant your seed in the growing media at the recommended depth as labelled. Most of this medium usage is universal for all the plants. Nutrient solution by the process of capillary moves up through the wick to deliver the nutrients and oxygen for the plant to thrive. You should beware that the wick system is advisable for beginners because of its simplicity and ease of assembling. Fast-growing plants such as lettuce and spinach, among others, perform better in the wick system.

Deep-Water Culture System: The netted pots already with holes can be used to make a simple deep-water culture system for placing the media. Drill a hole through a coffee container lid; align the netted-pot holes or slots to the holes on the coffee container. Make sure the pot can tightly enter the hole in the coffee container. Keep in mind that only one plant can slot in the coffee bottle; therefore, if you want to grow many plants, look for a bigger tote that can accommodate several pots.

The deep-water culture system integrates a tube through which air passes to the system. Carefully estimate 1.3 cm off the edge where you will make a provision for the air tube. Using a sharp knife slit the marked boundary. On the other side, slit another corner on the same container through which the pipe will pass.

Using a tube sized 0.64 – 1.27 cm, enter it through the slit you cut up to the bottom of the container. Remember to leave some length of the tube for connecting a bubbler (about 46 cm) on the top.

You should feed the container with purified water leaving an only quarter of the container unfilled. You can purchase already mixed nutrient solutions directly from an agricultural shop. You can alternatively establish the nutrients of each type of plant and intermix them by yourself while following the mixing guide enclosed in the box or marked on the container. Pouring too much water in the container will dilute the nutrient solution; therefore, strictly follow the container's instructions to measure the exact volume of water and how many nutrients to add. Once the right amount of nutrients is combined to the water in the container, stir it until the nutrients are evenly distributed in the water solution.

Using vermiculite or any other media, the net pot should be fully stuffed with the media. Cast the seeds in the media about 1.3 cm deeper. If you are not planting leafy crops, use transplanting instead of the seeds because seeds are only convenient for faster-growing plants and some herbs. Before you mess it all up, be advised that the seed depth fore mentioned is not a constant for every other plant. It varies from plant to plant. Do not hesitate to consult an expert. Never!

You can finally connect the air tube to the air machine to operationalize the system. The function of the bubbler machine should never be overlooked as it magnificently permits the dissolution of the air bubbles into oxygen, which eliminates the suffocation of your plants. Steadily brace the air tube end to end from the container to bubble machine to avoid air escape, which would reduce the amount of oxygen received by the plants, thereby drowning them. Finally, you can switch to your system. The growing media absorbs and transmits the nutrients to the plant roots and nourishes the plants. Like a wick system, the deep-culture method is preferred for quick maturing plants. Make sure the bubble machine does not shut down; otherwise, your plants can wither and dry out in a matter of hours.

Nutrient Film Technique (NFT): As the most common system used for hydroponics among growers, it is flexible and can be set-up anywhere. It can accommodate several NFT channels depending on the number of plants you want to grow. Because of the use of a solution pump, the NFT system functions like the Ebb and Flow Technique. In the NFT system, the principle of gravity is employed to direct the nutrient water solution to the water tank where the nutrient consistently runs in the system. The Nutrient Film System operates regularly using mobile components because it re-circulates the nutrient solution in the system frequently. It makes it conservative to water usage.

The underlying fundamental principle of a system is about the effectiveness of nutrient delivery to the entire plant root system. It is referred to as Film because it allows thin sized water to run over the root system instead of submerging the whole root system in the reservoir of water. Faster growing plants tend to thrive better in the Nutrient Film Technique system as opposed to larger plants with more significant roots. Lettuces, spinach, among many others, are examples of fast-growing plants as melons and squash are examples of plants with the larger plant. Fruity crops typically tomatoes may not correctly grow in this system if intensive care for them is not ensured.

Building the NFT system

Several possible ways exist to build a simple Nutrient Film Technique. It is important to note that all these ways are determined by the availability of space you choose from plants to cultivate. You should acquire the following items to build a super Nutrient Film Technique; NFT channel, reservoir (water tank), netted pots, air and water pump, air stone, etc.

The Reservoir

The poor-quality nutrient tank can cause serious leakages leading to insufficient supply of nutrients to the plant roots. Escape of air bubbles is a possibility, consequently drowning the plants. Therefore plastic reservoirs are recommended because when exposed to direct sun heat, it may not affect the water temperature as much as a metallic reservoir would. By the fact that you need to put your water tank below the running channel, pump the nutrient solution vertically into the channels for circulation in the system. You can use buckets and totes for placing your media and plants.

To the bottom of the reservoir, attach the pump with the air stone after creating a hole about 5.1 cm measured from the bottom of a 76-litter gallon or a tote. A sharp hard knife will do the job just fine. Determine one side of the tote for inserting the air stone. It should be at the very same with the hole for passing the tube that will carry the air. The pipe must directly be connected to the air pump.

Next to the reservoir, swamp the solution pump. The air pump should be opposite the air stone. From the bottom of the tote, you need to develop holes that are sufficient to pass the electric wires and a small tube. The small-sized tube should be approximately 1.3 cm lengthwise.

With 38 L, fully swamp the water pump in non-contaminant water together with the air stone that helps to create air bubbles, which consequently dissolve to form oxygen. Proceed to introduce your plant nutrient into the solution. Carefully follow how many nutrients you can add to how much volume of water to prevent dilution. Stir the solution until uniform saturation.

Using a smooth-surfaced PVC pipe, create a gentle slope into the channel. You can make the channel with sawhorses between which you can firmly place your tote over which you pass the PVC pipe.

Pots that will contain your plants should be fixed into the channel but firstly create holes on the upper side of the channel. Proper plant spacing is critical, and you, therefore, need to establish a spacing measurement of about 30 cm apart. This way, your plant root system can freely grow. After completing cutting holes on the upper side of the channel, you can install your pots, one in every hole but a range of 4 – 6 along every channel.

After installing the pots along the channel, design water emptying or re-circulation system at the bottom of the channel and on the top of the reservoir so that the reservoir will pump water from the top. In contrast, the channel drains it from the bottom side. The size of the hole at the bottom of the channel can be approximately 3.0 cm, and the one on the reservoir should be 4 cm ensuring the perfect re-circulation system.

Connect the nutrient solution tube in the middle of the channel and the other end of the channel. The holes should be sizable depending on the measurement of your tube so than the tubes are held firmly in a stable position.

At this point, you can now introduce your choice of growing media into the pots. Perlite, vermiculite is some of the commonly used media due to their high water retention capacity. Make sure the pots are stuffed up to three-quarters. You can plant the seeds 0.64 – 1.27 cm deep. Planting seeds directly into the soil is desired for quicker growing and leafy plants, including some herbs.

Finally, you can connect the water pump to deliver the nutrients' solution through the channel to the plant's root system. Avoid leakages in the channel, which wastes nutrients and oxygen. The water pump works with the help of a pump timer. Connect the pump timer and turn it on. The nutrient pump will automatically kick-start when the timer is switched and stops when the timer off. The timer turns on after every 3 hours.

Tips for productive plant growth using the Nutrient Film Technique System

However, to reap the most out of Nutrient Film Technique System in terms of higher productivity, you need to ensure the following.

Regulate your system temperature. Nutrient absorption is maximum at 65 – 68 Fahrenheit. This range of temperature is also best for oxygen dissolution.

Regularly calibrate your solution, which can double nutrient uptake by the plants enabling faster plant growth.

Frequently regulate your nutrient solution PH using a PH kit to maintain it within the ideal range of 5.8 – 6.3. Constant re-circulation of the Nutrient solution can potentially fluctuate its PH. It affects nutrient and oxygen uptake by the plants.

Periodically replace the nutrient in the solution. Much as growers using large tanks may not change their reservoir, but it is generally a good practice to change your reservoir before it is critical.

Do not expose your root system to light. Hide the root system in complete darkness to avoid the growth of algae, which deteriorates the plant growth rate.

Choose the perfect growing media so that it does not interrupt the root zone. Consequently, this can impact slower stunted growth.

Space your plants considerable to avoid overcrowding. This causes competition for nutrients and oxygen. The plant roots, when too congested, can potentially clog the channel, which affects the smooth flow of a film of water to nourish the roots.

Time and transfer the seedlings when its roots are fully developed and can survive out of the starter plug. Transplanting at the right time permits quick absorption of plant nutrients in the system.

Ebb and Flow System: Aquarium air pump, water pump, sturdy plastics for storage, pump timer, draining components, tubes are necessarily required for the locally made hydroponics system. All these components, apart from the fitting for the drainage system, can be hard to acquire.

Obtain two dark totes to ensure total darkness in the reservoir, which keeps the system algae free. Turn one of the totes to a tank in which air stones should be linked to the air pump to consistently produce air bubbles, which convert to oxygen in the nutrient water solution leading to optimal oxygenation crucial for plant survival. It is also in the reservoir that the water pump is place.

The second tote should firmly hold the containers in which plants will be introduced. Place the tote above the nutrient solution. Develop two holes on the bottom of the container, which will serve as appointing for fixing the drainage system and the flood for nourishing the plant roots.

Attach a tubing connecting a water pump, which floods the grow bed and a drainage fitting. Incorporate the timer by fixing the water pump to it. Feed the reservoir with approximately 10 gallons of water, and using the timer, you can control the water supply in the system as it re-circulates.

The container above the reservoir must always receive water first. It must not overflow, though. Through the tube, this water flows down to the entire system when the timer is switched on. The water passes to the selected media moistening it and the plant roots.

Ebb and Flow System is so simple and easy to make locally. Crop performance is excellent in terms of total output.

Multi-Pod Aeroponic System Design: In this Aeroponic system, the standard method is modified to a relatively more significant system. Holistically, to reduce and minimize the chances of nutrient deficiencies, use big water tanks. It is advisable to connect separate reservoirs to different water pumps if the water pump is weak. Still, for stronger ones, you just connect all repositories to the nutrient solution pump.

Hydroponic systems using the hybrid technique:
The hybrid system principally works on the fact that various hydroponic systems can be integrated and unified to form one better system. It uses a recovery technique where the nutrient solution consistently re-circulates through the system repeatedly until it is replaced with a new nutrient. Nutrient water solution washes the roots continuously in more profound depth. This system can be compared to two other hydroponic systems like the Nutrient Film Technique System and Deep-Water Culture System.

Hand Watering Technique: The hydroponic system is costly, especially initial costs and difficult to maintain. The hand-watering technique saves much of this cost, though it is tedious and tiresome to water the plants on time continuously.

Just Stuff bags with the soil-less mix, especially growing media like perlite and coconut coir to hold water, and the rest is easy. Fast draining media is not recommended for this technique of watering. It must drain the water slowly because the ultimate goal is to tell the nutrient solution for a longer time and stay moistened. For this method, you should create time and schedule for daily watering; otherwise, you stand to lose out all your plants as they will immediately dry and drown due to shortage of oxygen and nutrients.

Possible problems with hydroponic systems
The hydroponic system is an effective and efficient format for cultivating plants. The ease with which the systems are assembled makes it simpler to design it anywhere locally. However, hydroponic systems have several challenges that make it uneasy about using. It is, therefore, imperative to comprehend the drawbacks of this system to deal with them successfully.

Growth of algae: Algae being non-flowering waterweed, it is highly likely that algae will grow in your hydroponic water system, most notably in the reservoir and the tubing. A combination of water and sunlight or any light provides suitable environmental conditions for algae growth, so unfortunate. Isn't it? It sounds simple, but algae can cause a significant problem as dangerous as it is affecting plant root systems. Like your heart, the plant root system is the heart of it. Install an utterly dark-colored reservoir to seal light off the nutrient solution and always keep the reservoir closed.

Effectively, it is advisable to use lightproof material in your hydroponic system. The connection points of tubes to the holes are the main sections of possible leakages of light to the system. Equally, you can design the system to allow water to drip from beneath the cap that will block light though you may not see any blockage in the system due to obstruction. Also, accurately measure the size of the holes to fit in the media firmly.

System Leaks: It has been investigated that the pressure exerted in the reservoir and other parts of the hydroponic system directly causes leaks that develop in the system. Most of these leakages are as a result of drainage system fittings and emitters not firmly attached. High flowing water systems can also spill as it heats hardly on the root system. In systems that heavily rely on hydropower, power shutdowns can cause overflows in the nutrients reservoir, consequently drowning and suffocating plants.

However, such leakage challenges can be swiftly managed and controlled. Firstly, avoid using high-pressure water pumps unnecessarily. It is rare to find system tubes bursting when using low-pressure nutrient solution pumps. You can also create an additional nutrient tank that can adequately hold the water used in the entire system, and this can minimize the chances of an overflow. You can select the NFT system or Deep-Water Culture system because low-pressure pumps work just fine in them.

Clogs: The blockage of drainage tubes and other water circulation systems like sprays and drip is a common challenge experienced in all hydroponic systems. Tiny holes are used in spray systems like in Aeroponic systems and the Drip system. Of course, as small as they are, they can potentially clog at any one point during operations, especially if you are using impure water. Traces of salt can also accumulate, consequently blocking the tiny holes. Clogging the nutrient solution reduces the supply of nutrients and oxygen to the plant roots, causing plant malnutrition and reduced yield. Plants can dry out if there is an inadequate supply of water and oxygen. The use of nutrient filters can significantly minimize clogging. And you also need always to check and supervise the system to detect any faulty joints.

Convenience of use: Whereas the benefits of hydroponic systems are boundless, but the inconvenience that comes along with it can be unbearable such as daily supervision, regulating PH of the nutrient solution, temperature control, regularly cleaning the system. Tiny holes or spray nozzles and far to reach corners can be so tedious to clean due to there small size.

Nature of some systems: The total amount of time considerably spent in taking complete care of the system you have selected defines the temperamental nature of the system. Various systems need their solution level monitored, and if possible, replaced daily; otherwise, your plants will grow unhealthy. This affects their output. Systems like Aeroponics and Nutrient Film Technique System can suffer serious problems once the emitters are clogged, thus blocking the spray nozzles. Remember, plants grown hydroponically are very delicate, so they will surely die should thereby shortage of water supply and oxygen in the system.

If you are searching for reliable, reliable hydroponic systems, go for Deep-Water Culture System and Nutrient Film Technology because maintenance is easy. The frequency at which you check the system is only once the whole day.

Hydroponic hygiene: Tidiness is fundamental to the hydroponic system. Hydroponics systems require timely and frequent cleaning of the entire surrounding of the hydroponic system. A manifestation of diseases is extremely high if your system is untidy, and its spread escalates faster in a dirty environment. Weeds like algae thrive in wet conditions combined with light. Cleanliness can eliminate the growth of algae and the unnecessary outbreak of pests and diseases. However, bacteria that help in plant growth can be supported to grow in your system. You should monitor it closely to suppress the emergence of pathogenic organisms harmful to your plants. The only successful way to do that is to keep clean at all times, dry out the spills of water that can potentially breed these pathogens.

The health of your plants: It can be a little hard to detect arising health issues in a hydroponic system because many growers think hydroponically grown plants are always healthy; they are ever taken unaware when plants' health begins to deteriorate. At this point, plant production will already be affected. Frequent monitoring is critical as it helps to quickly identify signs and symptoms and treat it when still early before spreading.

Failure to lean as you grow plants: The most annoying issue in hydroponics is that all individual plants have different properties, and how they respond to a particular system. That's explicitly why some plants don't do well in other systems and well in others, e.g., fruity plants perform poorly in drip systems, whereas leafy plants thrive in it. Growers coherently have not taken time to review their previous procedures that would improve their next harvest.

PH level regulation: The PH of your nutrient solution is a vital determinant of how your plants will yield or how healthy they can be. Unlike in organic soil where the PH is automatically regulated, hydroponic technology requires frequent adjusting of the solution PH due to the solution's re-circulation. The land is a natural PH buffer. Fluctuating nutrient solution PH can be realized every hour, depending on the absorption rate and temperature changes. You need to watch your solution PH many times a day; otherwise, your plants can perish.

Nutrient Deficiency: Plants in hydroponics suffer from deficiencies and dangerous conditions that arise over time. This is not even challenging, and the most challenging part is identifying the distinct nutrient lacking in the solution. By the time you recognize the nutrient lacking, the plant would have grievously suffered damaging malnutrition. Things like human error, plant growth, PH, among others, can contribute to deficiencies and toxicity. Immediately clean the system should you identify shortcomings in the system.

Using hard water in the system: Hard water is likely to give birth to some challenges in your hydroponic system. Firstly there are a lot of particles in the hard water mainly it is from the tap, and these dissolved particles can build up in your drainage system and drip system, thereby reducing efficiency in delivering nutrients to the plant root system. Secondly, tap water has some minerals, and it is hard to establish how much of those minerals are present in your solution. It leads to a nutrient imbalance in your solution. The minerals include magnesium and calcium salts.

Blocked or broken pumps and nozzles: The use of water in hydroponics means tubes and nozzles are required to deliver water from one point to the other. The pipes and spray nozzles used are prone to blockages and breakages, resulting in flooding and a shortage of nutrients and oxygen to the plant roots. Systems that use spray nozzles like in Aeroponics clogging is common as a pile of salt bocks the system hence suffocating the plants.

Wrong choice of growing media: There are many choices of growing media, depending on the type of plant you want to grow. However, these mediums have different nutrient absorption and retention capacity. Selecting a wrong growing media can doom all your plants. For instance, you need to use porous growing media for fruity plants because they need more water than fast-growing plants. You should know well in advance, which growing media you can reuse and which one you need to trash after using once.

Plant disease: Much as it is true that diseases are less likely to attach hydroponically grown plants, they can equally suffer from diseases if hydroponic hygiene is not clean. Uncontrolled temperatures, water spillage, sunlight, humidity can cause disease outbreaks, mention it. You should always be precautious because the outbreak of diseases in a hydroponic system can spread more rapidly when compared to plants grown in traditional gardens. Plants in the hydroponic system are close and use a single reservoir to draw nutrients and oxygen from, a factor that escalates the spreading of diseases.

Therefore, hydroponic technology has many systems for cultivating plants. Each system is unique in its setting, and growers can benefit from all of them, given their unique advantages like faster plant growth and frequent harvests throughout the year. However, as discussed above, hydroponic systems have several challenges and setbacks that make it unreliable. But doing a few things right can fix the problems associated with hydroponic technology.

CHAPTER SIX

Tricks to grow plants better, Mistakes to avoid in Hydroponics

Tricks to grow plants better

As we have seen in all the previous chapters, hydroponic technology is an impressively reliable technology for faster quality plant growth, doubled total harvest, and increased flexibility of the system as it can practically be established anywhere. Given growers have the right intermix of vital plant requirements, growing media, and correctly managed the other environmental factors such as temperature, lighting, humidity, solution PH, excellent plant health and growth is guaranteed. It has impacted several growers to shift from traditional gardening to hydroponic technology. However, this is only possible if growers do not neglect the following best hydroponic growing tips.

Ensure water quality: Knowing the exact quality of the kind of water you are using in your hydroponic system is essential. Hard water and tap water are not pure. It contains some minerals and chemicals that may cause an imbalance of your nutrient solution. Aspects of solution PH can be altered if you don't test your water quality. The use of a PH strip measures the PH. Optimal PH level is between 5.5 and 6.5, but the kind of plant growth can dictate this. It is highly advisable to disinfect and treat your water before exposing your plants to it in the system; otherwise, you are most likely to encounter disastrous challenges like an outbreak of diseases.

Regulate your water temperature between 68 Fahrenheit and 72 Fahrenheit. Water chillers and heaters are available in stores to regulate the temperature of your nutrient water solution. Plant root's capacity to absorb water can be affected by the water temperature, consequently impacting plant overall plant growth. Some plants perform better in worm condition than others in cold conditions. So be mindful of the heat of the choice of plant you are growing in your system.

Use a fertigation system: To further boost the rate of plant growth, you can inject the right type of fertilizer into your hydroponic system. In traditional gardening, fertilizers can be applied in the soil, but for hydroponic systems, liquid fertilizers are introduced directly to plant roots by injecting them in the nutrient reservoir. Exposing the plant roots to too much fertilizer can instantly kill the plants. Also, beware that establishing the correct volume of compost is complicated more, so balancing the PH during fertilizer application is challenging too, or else nutrient absorption by the roots can be affected.

You should not stop to regulate your PH level, and in fact, fertigation requires more frequent PH monitoring and adjusting. Installation of the fertilizer application system is more convenient and efficient for feeding the fertilizers into the system. It also ensures even circulation of that fertilizer in the order. The most typical mistake growers make the failure to match the correct amount of fertilizer to the amount of nutrient solution and constant adjustment of the PH to the ideal levels.

Consequently, calibration of the equipment allows for the proper balance between these elements, thus optimal growth.

Select the right growing media: In a soil-less cultivation system like Hydroponics, sufficient flow of water and nutrients is aided by the use of a growing media such as vermiculite, coconut coir mention it, which retains and transmits nutrient solution to the plant roots. Choosing the right growing media permits an excellent balance between moisture and oxygen, so you should select the right media.

At times, you need to integrate two or more media in a single hydroponic system. Such a combination is known to have more efficient and higher oxygen and nutrient solution retention capacity. You can be assured with constant nourishment of plant roots. Thus a better performance of your crops guaranteeing higher yields. Commonly clay pebbles are used to perfect retention of the nutrient solution. Coco coir, you can equally use Rockwool as growing media. Therefore, to enhance your plant's overall performance of your plants, you need to pick the right media after analyzing the water requirements enough to sustain your plant optimally. The wrong choice of growing media can result in suffocation and drying of your plant due to an insufficient supply of oxygen and nutrient solution.

Cleaning the system: The untidy hydroponic system and its surrounding can significantly impact the performance of your plants. The unclean system will compromise the overall function of your system by potentially breeding pests, diseases, and algae. Your plants are likely to perish once infested with bugs but most imperatively affecting the crops. By all means possible, you regularly have to disinfect, clean, and keep your system dry by checking for any leakages and weak points.

Your nutrient reservoir is a critical point where potential pathogens can breed and harbour. To avoid this from happening, regularly decontaminate your system timely. You can draw a precise schedule to implement this. Some growers use bleaching solutions after emptying the reservoir you firstly need to leave the tank and only fill it halfway. The eluded bleaching agent aids dissolution of any particles that may clog the system, causing more problems. Don't take so long without cleaning your reservoir; you can program to sterilize it once every week.

Most plants do not perform in the hydroponic system because of insufficient supply of nutrients and oxygen. It mainly occurs either due to clogged tubes or the use of the wrong growing media. Making sure your system is cleared of any accumulation in the drainage system ensures an adequate supply of water and oxygen. It fosters plant growth.

Lighting system: Don't get it wrong. Sunlight is vital for plant life, whether grown in soil or water (soil-less media, Hydroponics). Though light as a growth requirement for plants varies from one to another, some plants need more light than others. For example, vegetables like tomatoes and some flowering plants demand more lighting up to six hours in twenty-four hours. For growers in a location that receives less or no natural light can alternatively improvise by installing the artificially manufactured lighting system. The first step is to know the light requirement of the kind of plant grown.

PH level: Plants' ability to absorb certain plant minerals and nutrients such as carbohydrates and vitamins is highly dictated by the alkalinity and acidity of the nutrient solution. The PH level of your answer depends on the kind of plant you have grown in your system. High PH level is not suitable for herbs, so they will not thrive. Consequently, identify the PH requirement for the individual type of plants you intend to grow to harvest quality and higher yields.

Nutrient solution temperature: Temperature is critical as plant growth diminishes faster when temperatures rise high up to 80 degrees. Temperature is bound to rise and fall due to several factors like heating bulbs installed in the system, the weather in the outdoor environment, and heat generated by the running pumps. It is this that makes temperature control a considerable challenge. To avoid this, you can install a cooling system that will blow in cold air whenever it goes up or buy a fan. The most effective alternative is for you to continually shift your system indoor when it gets too cold or hot outdoor. This depends on the type of plants grown, though. Plants generally thrive in warm temperatures, as discussed in chapter two.

Having a plan: Just like how a business without a business plan is most likely to fail, indulging in hydroponic cultivation without proper planning cannot yield the desired success. You need to establish all the essential plant requirements, identify a suitable location, know the photoperiod, get a PH adjuster, and obtain the types of equipment necessary. Not to miss acquiring any critical components, you need to list down all of them. Before starting your operation, schedule a maintenance program such as nutrient feeding, cleaning, and emptying the reservoir, among others. If you don't have a concrete plan for your operation, you are bound to fail.

Feeding nutrients: You stand to feed your plants with the wrong nutrients if you do not identify the kind of particular nutrients they require to grow. If you are not sure about the type of nutrients to use, do not hesitate to consult a plant nutritionist or an experienced hydroponic grower. But it is equally crucial for you to have the correct nutrient measuring equipment; otherwise, re-feeding can become problematic.

It is not highly recommended to intermix plant nutrients by yourself but instead, buying an already mixed solution is the best to begin. As you gain experience, you can then try to customize your nutrients. Some growers prefer to use an additive to boost plant growth. However, additives can compromise the growth of your plants. Sticking to standard nutrients is the best as long as you follow the instructions that come along with the nutrients and regulate environmental conditions like humidity, temperature, solution PH, lighting, refilling the reservoir, constant supply of oxygen as well as keeping plant roots moist can give you a good the result. As nutrients are changed all the time, it is a good practice to clean the entire reservoir thoroughly before introducing a new nutrient to avoid contamination. To eliminate inconveniences, you can install two tanks so that you will be merely switching from one to the other.

Root health: Of course, no plant can survive without their roots, and definitely cannot thrive, can it? No! To prevent damages to your plant roots, you need to schedule a timetable that will allow watching plant root's health frequently. Healthy plant roots impact on their ability to absorb nutrients delivered to them. Do you usually have an appetite when you are suffering from Malaria? No, I don't think so. So, it is just the same with plants. Other precautions that will ensure continued plant root's health is obstruction of light into their roots system or in the reservoir as light with water can lead to the development of algae. Dangerous for plant roots.

Photoperiod manipulation: Light is essential to plants, including sparking off flowering in them. They need shorter exposure to light, though. You have to comprehend the light needs of your plant and then schedule a lighting program so that you can switch on the lights when it time to turn them on and reverse is real. Using a timer could work just fine. However, if your system is using an artificial lighting system, you need to protect the plants from light when it is time to switch off the lights. Your lighting system can sensitively influence plant production. Therefore, it is best to ensure consistency in lighting.

The right tools and equipment to use: Lacking vital hydroponic tools can halt the entire operation hence the need first to obtain all the essential equipment before you launch your system. Types of equipment like black or opaque reservoir, lighting system, various plant nutrients, fan system, PH adjusting kit, temperature gauge, etc. need to be available. All these types of equipment play vital roles in the hydroponic system; any of them can be overlooked. You can ably manage the conditions of the entire system with these tools and be assured of faster growth and many harvests in a year.

Decide what to grow: The beauty with the hydroponic system is that it can be customized to grow almost every other plant. The difference is in the variation of nutrient requirements and the distinct environmental conditions that suit each plant. Larger plants precisely have unique properties as opposed to smaller plants. For instance, larger plants require more water to thrive, and the opposite is exact with small plants, other plants perform better in acidic conditions while others do not. You need to understand all plant needs or at least the ones you intend to grow, but herbs and vegetables would be the right choice for beginners as they are not very to maintain.

Summary of best-growing tip for Hydroponics
Here is an overall summary of how you can successfully grow plants in your hydroponic system without encountering too many challenges.

- Carefully identify your equipment requirements
- Establish nutrients necessary for your plant growth
- Understand lighting requirements for your plant
- Avoid as much as possible to use additive in your nutrient solution
- Develop a plan for managing your system in terms of feeding
- Ensure total darkness in the reservoir to avoid the growth of algae
- Disinfect and decontaminate your system regularly
- Empty your reservoir regularly
- Keep pets out
- Check your solution PH regularly
- Watch out for leakages in your system by supervision
- Use the right growing media
- Ensure constant watering
- Avail enough oxygen

Mistakes growers need to avoid

Undoubtedly, various people pursue Hydroponics for a variety of purposes, ranging from financial reasons to hobbies. But anyhow, the bottom line is ultimately doing the right things because whether your motivation to do it as a hobby or generate revenue, you need to succeed in it. Prior know-how and extensive planning are outstanding to the realization of any form of success in Hydroponics. The slightest mistake in a hydroponic system can prove so costly, which on an unfortunate notice, is common among young growers even experienced one too sometimes. Therefore, I thought it would be helpful to share some of the common mistakes growers make, which affects their overall production capacity and reduces their profit margin every time and then. Below are the mistakes hydroponic growers make.

Failure to measure solution PH on time: PH monitoring and adjusting aspects of water solution cannot be ignored in any circumstance. The too acidic nutrient solution can result in roasting your plant roots. For what benefit would that to you? Besides, plants need moderate PH to aid the absorption of vitamins and carbohydrates, among many others. It is a must for you to purchase at least one PH testing kit to check PH levels every other time. Perfect PH level provides a conducive environment for impressive plant performance.

Compromising photosynthesis: Every single plant needs to manufacture their food through photosynthesis or at least compliment the food they have been fed the water solution. So in a hydroponic setting, artificial lighting systems have to be installed if your plants cannot access natural sunlight. Light is also essential for the flowering and fruiting of plants. Gone are the days when sunlight was the only source of lighting for gardening; today, LED light can be found almost in every store. Stop excusing yourself, get that LED, and install it in your system because your plants need it.

Creation of a toxic environment: Your plant will, of course, nourish and healthily grow in a tidy environment. Generally, hydroponic elements such as oxygen, nutrients, water mention it, have to be fed when they are known to be clean because pollutants are always present, especially in the water solution. Pests and diseases love dirt as a breeding ground. You need to treat and disinfect your system on a regular schedule. New growers like using cheap fertilizers that contain harmful toxins that directly attack the plant root system. Besides, fungus and algae love humid conditions with exposure to light; algae will grow in your system, destroying your plant root system.

Poor planning of your grow space: A common mistake growers make is often to set up in locations with limited space. It is good to start small, but it is better to leave an expansion allowance. Besides, if you are growing large plants like melons and pumpkins, you need to secure a big space; otherwise, the plants will squeeze up in that little area and won't yield well. You need to forecast your space requirement for the next six to five years, especially if you are a commercial grower. Extensive research and planning can help you to avoid making this mistake over and again.

Losing attention: Many growers are always very excited in the first few weeks of operating their hydroponic garden. They commit so much time to the success of their garden. However, as they continue, the time, attention, and commitment to their plants drastically reduce or, at times, disappears completely. Not that whatever it is you want to achieve by investing in hydroponic growing cannot happen overnight. In any event, you need to keep a close eye to succeed consistently. Monitoring PH level, temperature, light, nutrient replacement, and watching out for faults in the system are crucial. You can achieve that if you give your plants attention, including spotting out sick and malnourished plants.

Air allowance inside the system: Most farmers make a mistake of unknowingly suffocating their plants with insufficient air. Growers need to understand that air is critical to daily plant survival, just as we need oxygen to survive. Don't we? The mixture of oxygen and carbon dioxide should be adequate in your garden as long as they are free from industrial pollutants your plants will thrive. Plants can suffer from airborne diseases if the air is contaminated. Coherently, you will need to install proper ventilation or air conditioning system because, at times, placing a fan in the room may not even be sufficient enough. Active circulation of air in your hydroponic system helps to regulate the temperature inside your grow room. Hot temperatures can kill your plants or affect the quality of yield produced as well as stagnate their growth and causing severe dehydration of your plants.

Hard to use systems: As we have seen before, hydroponic systems can be tailored and customized to fit anywhere. The mistake growers make is that they tend to design their system in the way it creates becomes challenging and difficult to maintain. Make sure your system has a space allowance to allow free movement and possibly expand in the future. Poor setups often result in difficulties in harvesting, inability to control pests and diseases, among others.

Overlooking system build costs: Growers sometimes underestimate the initial system set up cost implications on their budget. They forget that even after your order is up and running, they will incur maintenance costs such as replacing broken pipes, disinfecting the system, pest and disease control, replacing blown bulbs, and restocking of nutrients. They often find themselves stranded without cash. It is essential to realize that various systems have cost implications. Others do not require some components to function appropriately while others do. It is good you identify your equipment requirements depending on the method you prefer to use and draw a complete cost structure for the system. Just imagine your run out of cash when you needed to replace the nutrients or the air pump. Won't your crops be doomed?

Wrong choice of plants to grow: Every plant has a distinct property and therefore, will react differently in every hydroponic technique used to grow them. Where you intend to locate your hydroponic system is very important in selecting the plants to build. Individual plants will not just thrive in any condition. You are having the right answers to questions like which type of plant can grow in your system? What is the nature of the climate of that area? For instance, you cannot grow plants that require cold conditions in a tropical environment; you cannot grow tomatoes in a raft system because it does not require too much water. Therefore only you cannot fail if you choose the right plants for the right hydroponic system.

Using the wrong nutrients: To enhance rapid plant growth, growers add additional fertilizers. The mistake is that they do not comprehend what is in conventional fertilizers. Particles in natural manure are resistant to dissolve, or at least some particles will not dissolve in your solution. Small solid particles in typical fertilizer can quickly build up and clog the small tubes as well as spray nozzles wielded in Aeroponics to discharge nutrient solution to the plant in a mist form. Additives in your nutrient solution can cause imbalance, consequently causing nutrient deficiencies in your hydroponic nutrient solution. Much as growers are to blame for this, nutrient and fertilizer manufacturers also take a portion of the blame as well as because they also sell their product with a mixing manual. Still, for small farmers, their nutrient recommended dosage could be too much.

Watering too often: It is no question that plants need water to grow; at least most people know about it. Still, the commonest mistake growers make often overwatering, leading to the waterlogged hydroponic environment. Keeping your hydroponic environment watery can cause a set of severe problems to your plants like root and root rotting, creating a breeding ground for pests and diseases and growing algae, especially if the water is exposed to light. You can try to clean up such messes by allowing evaporation of the excess water. You can come up with the proper watering program and stick to it. To find out if your plants need watering, you can simply tap the growing media. Moist growing media means watering is not yet required, but when the ever-increasing media feels dry, and then know it is time to do some watering for your plants.

Insufficient lighting: In any hydroponic system, a lighting system is one critical aspect. At times hydroponic growers invest in the wrong type of lighting system, thereby interrupting the photosynthesis process. The variety of hydroponic lighting systems out there can make it challenging to pick the correct one for your system. The wrong choice of lighting system is, no doubt, a path to failure. The complications your plants are exposed to due to poor lighting include growth deficiency, poor or no fruit yields, among others. Understanding the amount of light the kind of plant you are growing is essential in picking the right lights for them. Some of the available lightings include but not limited to fluorescent lighting, HID lights, and LED lights, among others.

Ventilation: This is a factor that calls for even closure attention as it affects many other elements of the hydroponic system. First of all, sufficient ventilation impacts the system's temperature levels by either increasing your nutrient solution temperature or lowering it considerably to critical levels. If your system is situated in desert-like weather, then you need to have enough ventilation to cool the solution. Simultaneously, for cold areas, you need to close up a ventilation system to prevent the possibility of your plant roots freezing. Additionally, you will need to have adequate ventilation for plants that thrive in cold conditions, and the reverse is valid for a plant that performs well in warm conditions. For ventilation, you can simply choose to create more openings on the wall or the roof, or you can install an air conditioning system if your budget allows.

Sanitation of your system: Keeping your system clean can be very tedious; as a result, many growers tend to ignore their hydroponic system sanitation in a few weeks or months of running the system. Your hydroponic system is quite extensive rather than only your plants; it involves the floor, types of equipment. But poor sanitation in your system can prove more hazardous than you probably think. Once there is an outbreak of diseases, it can spread more rapidly as compared to the one in traditional gardening due to the close spacing of plants in a hydroponic setting. Besides, plants share nutrients from a single reservoir, which also re-circulates in the entire system, thus fostering quicker spreading. To eliminate or avert such problems, you need to frequently clean and dry the garden room, occasionally empty or replace the nutrients in the reservoir, and flushing the entire system.

All in all, the world is swiftly shifting crop production from traditional gardening to hydroponic farming. The hydroponic system has time and over again proven to be the most reliable source of crop production because of high yield that is an association with the hydroponic system. The world needs a constant supply of food to sustain its population that is ever-growing day by day adequately. Although the advantages of the hydroponic system outweigh the ones of traditional gardening, improper management in terms of controlling environmental aspects such as temperature, lighting, oxygen, humidity, among others, plants grown hydroponically can all perish and die within no time. Therefore, to maximize hydroponic crop production, you need to be vigilant and choose the right type of hydroponic system that can suit the plant you intend to grow.